THE UPSIDE OF BEING DOWN

THE UPSIDE OF BEING DOWN

JEN GOTCH

with Rachel Bertsche

GALLERY BOOKS

New York   London   Toronto   Sydney   New Delhi

Gallery Books
An Imprint of Simon & Schuster, Inc.
1230 Avenue of the Americas
New York, NY 10020

First Gallery Books hardcover edition March 2020

GALLERY BOOKS and colophon are registered trademarks of
Simon & Schuster, Inc.

For information about special discounts for bulk purchases,
please contact Simon & Schuster Special Sales at 1-866-506-1949 or
business@simonandschuster.com.

The Simon & Schuster Speakers Bureau can bring authors to your
live event. For more information or to book an event, contact the
Simon & Schuster Speakers Bureau at 1-866-248-3049 or visit
our website at www.simonspeakers.com.

Interior design by Alexis Minieri

Manufactured in the United States of America

1   3   5   7   9   10   8   6   4   2

Library of Congress Cataloging-in-Publication Data

Names: Gotch, Jen, 1971– author.
Title: The upside of being down : how mental health struggles led to my
greatest successes in work and life / Jen Gotch.
Description: First Gallery Books hardcover edition. | New York : Gallery
Books, 2020.
Identifiers: LCCN 2019045250 (print) | LCCN 2019045251 (ebook) | ISBN
9781982108816 (hardcover) | ISBN 9781982108830 (ebook)
Subjects: LCSH: Gotch, Jen. | Businesspeople—United States—Biography. |
Businesswomen—United States—Biography. | Manic-depressive
persons—United States—Biography. | Creative ability—United States. |
Business women—Mental health—United States.
Classification: LCC HC102.5.G675 A3 2020 (print) | LCC HC102.5.G675
(ebook) | DDC 616.89/50092 [B]—dc23
LC record available at https://lccn.loc.gov/2019045250
LC ebook record available at https://lccn.loc.gov/2019045251

ISBN 978-1-9821-0881-6
ISBN 978-1-9821-0883-0 (ebook)

For my parents, who have never stopped offering emotional support or encouragement, and selflessly financed the first thirty years of my life, even though they only signed on for eighteen. (Guys, you need a new agent; you really got taken for a ride.)

Contents

Contents

Introduction

Here's the thing about writing a memoir: the person you are when you start and the person you are when you finish are practically strangers. It's like those before and after pictures on makeover shows, except all the transformation happens on the inside. Well, my hair got longer too, but you know what I mean.

Writing this book has changed me. There has been so much learning involved, especially about myself, and it has required a depth of introspection and emotional excavation that I sure as hell didn't anticipate when I signed on for the job. In writing chapters about my childhood and my family and my marriage and my ego, I was forced to ask myself some tough questions—*Why did I feel that way? What was I really yearning for in that moment/ relationship/job? What went wrong? How much of the blame did I need to own?* The answers weren't always pretty, and accepting responsibility in failed relationships can be hard, although important. At points throughout the last year, the difficulty of this endeavor pushed me to some low places, full of frustration and self-doubt, and left me feeling defeated. But now that I've landed on the other side, I feel stronger than I have in years. I'm more self-aware, hopeful, and content . . . and frankly a hell of a lot less anxious than I ever could have envisioned. It's been a fitting journey for a book called *The Upside of Being Down*, a manifestation of the fact that our struggles can lead to our greatest successes, and I am so excited to share what I've learned with you in the process of this book and of my life.

I have wanted to write a book since I was a tiny sun-kissed six-year-old in Boca Raton, Florida, propped up on phone books so I could reach the typewriter (yes, a type-writer, it was the seventies, that's what we typed on). Little Jen, with her blond pigtails and tan skin and incredibly hairy arms, almost always wearing a sundress—blue with swiss dots, maybe, or white with lace trim—banging away at the keyboard in her father's office, drafting the story of a princess who lived among polka-dot mushrooms in a faraway land filled with glitter, unicorns, and rainbows. It was destined to be a bestseller. The final product of all this typing was less intelligible and more like a series of random letters jammed up against each other, but the story I was trying to convey was definitely the one I just mentioned. But I didn't know how to type—or spell—yet. I put the book on hold for a while (and by a while I mean forty years), but somewhere in the midst of growing up and moving away and changing careers and changing again and going to therapy and managing my mental health and starting a company and then selling a company, I found my voice. It was my voice and vision that helped launch and grow ban.do, the bright, optimistic multimillion-dollar lifestyle company where I am now chief creative officer. It was my voice on my podcast, *Jen Gotch is OK . . . Sometimes*, which is where I first really dug into my struggles with mental health (though my Instagram followers know I've been sharing that part of me for years) and let listeners in on my spirited yet very one-sided conversations with my dog, Phil, and my cat, Gertie. And it's my voice that will drive this story—now with fewer unicorns and rainbows but much improved spelling—as I take you through my own winding journey in an effort to help you navigate yours.

In the course of my life, I have been diagnosed with bipolar disorder, generalized anxiety, and ADD. I feel like there's also some lactose intolerance in there, but who's to say? My success has come in tandem with these diagnoses—sometimes despite them, other times because of them. You're probably used to seeing creative types depicted as successful or suffering, one or the other. My story is both.

I've considered my mental health struggles a gift ever since someone first put a name to them in my early twenties. Before that they were truly a pain in the ass, but once I understood and had a vocabulary for what I was dealing with, I found strength and empathy and patience. Calling on these traits isn't always easy, and I am not in limitless supply (because, who is?) but I have enough on reserve and know how to access them when I need to, thanks to a lot of hard work and self-reflection. Developing an appreciation for the importance of being mentally healthy has helped me run a company that encourages emotions in the workplace (wild concept, right?) and that operates as a group of humans rather than a corporate conglomerate. Ban.do's tagline is "We exist to help you be your best" and that's the mission that drives the company. Learning about mental health has taught me that living your life with hope, optimism, lightheartedness, and humor (lots and lots of humor) is a tremendous gift you can give yourself. I know now that you can suffer from mental illness and still maintain good mental health, and that the reverse is also true. You can have zero diagnosed mental illnesses, but if you ignore your emotional well-being, you will never be mentally strong and you'll also miss out on a lot of the joy that comes with being human.

Fifteen(ish) years ago, I was sitting on the couch during a therapy appointment, and my long-standing psychologist predicted I would become a mental health advocate.

"How would I do that?" I asked. "No one knows who I am—how would they even find me?" This was well before Instagram, and probably even before Myspace.

"I could see you speaking at conferences, sharing your struggles and successes," she said.

The thought of speaking in front of more than three people instantly made me want to turn to dust, yet her prediction wedged itself into the back of my mind. It sounded scary and embarrassing, but then over a decade later, I started expressing myself. First, at small conferences, just like she said, and then eventually on larger platforms. I was talking about mental illness on my Instagram Stories and my podcast and creating jewelry at ban.do to raise awareness about mental health. And while plenty of times over the years I was so turned off by my own voice that I wanted to murder it via multiple maiming stabs of the tongue, or maybe removal of the throat organs altogether (that's possible, right?), the response was overwhelming. As it turns out, I am not the only person who deals with these issues on a daily basis. That was strangely surprising for me, but if you struggle with any of this you know how isolating and singular your experience can feel.

Since this book will address issues of mental health head-on, we should probably get something out of the way: I am not a doctor. I am the founder and creative lead at a lifestyle company that sells disco balls you can drink out of and bath mats with boobs on them. Oh, and when I refer to my "research," please know that in most cases I'm talking about a quick Google search and anywhere from five to seventeen minutes of reading articles on *Psychology Today*. What I'm saying is, as much as I wish I could, I'm not here to diagnose you or suggest a treatment plan. I'm instead going to share my experiences as a layperson—without getting too clinical—and hope that in doing so, I can help you tune into your own experiences and feel less alone. I hope this goes without saying, but just in case: If you suspect you are suffering from a mental health issue, please seek out the help of an actual professional.

I was in a sorority in college. That often comes as a surprise to people, so imagine how they react when I tell them I was actually the president. Regardless, during rush week, we put on a talent show. There was singing and dancing, sure, and there might have even been a magic show, but for reasons I will never understand, we also showed off our talent for reading philosophy. I have no idea how that qualifies as a talent, but it's not really the point of the story so let's just go with it. In this portion of the show, one of my sorority sisters stood on the stage wearing a pair of giant glasses that seemed to turn her regular eyes into the cartoon googly version. She held a giant leather-bound gold-embossed book and pretended to read from it. In total monotone, she declared: " 'The unexamined life is not worth living.' " Then she definitively slammed the book shut. Just to dial up the drama, we put baby powder inside the book so that when it closed a cloud of "dust" came out, a reminder that this was an old, wise book.

I've been thinking about that sorority performance a

lot since I started writing this book, since here I am living the examined life. It really does feel worthwhile. I never thought that, in my forties, I'd be garnering wisdom from a rush week talent show, but I don't turn my nose up at a good life lesson, no matter how unlikely the source—proof that I too am old and wise. And if you squeeze me really hard, I swear dust appears.

My goal with this book is to share my story—of growing up and finding myself and success and failure and self-doubt and family and dancing and eating and aging—because it probably isn't that different from yours. We all eventually live some version of that narrative. So this is not a cautionary tale; there is nothing to pity. Life happens—and you look at it and you learn from it or you don't, and you enjoy it or you don't. At forty-seven, I am enjoying it more than ever, and I hope you will too. And if reading this book helps you skip a couple of these chapters in your own life (specifically the darker ones), and you walk away with increased self-awareness and strong emotional intelligence, then I'll call that a major win.

My dad, on the other hand, will only consider this book a major win if it gets him more Instagram followers.

Chapter 1

It's Not Easy Being Green

I remember having the distinct feeling, for at least two days, that my skin had changed color. It went from my healthy, normal flesh tone to green. Not bright green, but green-tinged. More lip stain than lipstick. Regardless, it was green enough that I was really confused when no one in my family seemed to be concerned about my health, because I WAS GREEN, and going from a normal human color to green should probably at least provoke an "are you okay?" from the people who claim to love you. But nothing? Were they ignoring me . . . again?

You're probably wondering why I was starting to veer

into Shrek territory—or at least why I thought I was. Let me give you a little backstory.

I graduated from Florida State in December 1993, a year and a half before the skin incident, and made the bold decision to move to Atlanta to start my life as a full-fledged grown-up. (At the time, when you graduated from FSU and wanted to head to the big city, that big city was usually Atlanta.) I wanted to be excited—this was the beginning of the rest of my life—but in reality I was scared. I was not emotionally, mentally, or professionally prepared for the real world, and deep down I knew that.

I was smart, but I had a limited professional skill set and a degree in literature and philosophy—a degree the job market was not begging for. My first plan was to get by on temp work, an incredibly specific and effective form of torture. No, seriously, if you've never done it, just for fun, try walking into an office full of strangers who are well trained in their jobs and know each other's names and how to work the copy machine, and then quietly, without making any sudden movements, sit yourself down at the front desk—the FUCKING LIFELINE of the office—and start answering the phones. It's a hoot, a real hoot. I did not last long as a temp, and instead of responsibly looking for another job, I sat alone in my room for what felt like days at a time (my friend Forrest, who lived with me in Atlanta, says it was more like hours at a time, but it sure felt like days), interrupted only by weekends when I would travel back to FSU to get drunk and make out. The bulk of my time in Atlanta was spent speed-eating cereal because we all know what a total letdown soggy cereal is. In retrospect, the most productive thing I did during those months was learn all the lyrics to "Shoop" by Salt-N-Pepa. (I can still sing it to this day. People find it really cool; no, I made that up, most people are annoyed by it, but one person found it cool.)

Adding to this quarter-life crisis was the fact that a few weeks before graduation, I made what would be a pivotal decision to go on the birth control pill. Today that might seem like a really small thing, but in the early nineties the pill was way more intense than it is today. It could really fuck with your hormones, or even cause a chemical imbalance in your brain that would negatively affect your mental health. (I should add that this decision made no sense, as I'd just broken up with my college boyfriend and had literally zero intention of having sex with anyone. Kissing, yes; sex, no. But being on the pill was cool and grown-up, and there was a chance it might even give me bigger boobs, so I went for it.)

So yeah, after halfheartedly trying to be a functioning grown-up, the uncertainty and fear coupled with the side effects of the pill incited a slow but dramatic spiral that started as emotional eating and weight gain—hello, crispy cereal!—but eventually revealed the bigger issues: self-loathing, generalized anxiety, and the intensification of my undiagnosed clinical depression. Of course, I didn't know all this at the time, hence the *undiagnosed* part. What I knew then was that I felt lost, overwhelmed, and completely paralyzed by the mere concept of growing up. I knew in my gut that I needed help, and that I was not going to get that help in Atlanta. Certainly not when I could remain in denial, eating cereal, learning hip-hop lyrics, and bar hopping with friends.

So, under the pretense of wanting to save money, I accepted defeat and moved home.

I can't say for sure if it was the hormone altering of the pill, or the relative safety of being in my childhood home, or the last twenty-three years of trying to manage a psychological imbalance coming to a head, but soon after moving home, my brain just couldn't take it anymore.

And the first big sign—or at least the first noticeable one—was that I believed, with all my heart, that my skin had turned green.

Today, twenty-five-ish years later, it's tempting to take some major creative liberties with the next part of this story, because there are some gaps in my memory, but the truth is fucked-up enough without having to make stuff up, so I'm just going to tell you what I remember. My memory is sometimes unreliable, but my heart is always in the right place.

My parents weren't ignorant jerks—they had working eyes—and despite our differences I knew they loved me dearly, so their disinterest in my new green hue was incredibly frustrating. One afternoon I pulled my mom into the bathroom, I guess assuming that the lighting in there was better. (We always go into the bathroom for better light, but is it actually any better? And if it is, why don't we just use that lighting scheme throughout the house? I digress. It's what I do—weeeeeeeeeeeeeeeeeeeee.) I shoved my arm in her face.

"Look at it. Look at it. It's green. It's definitely green!"

"Ummmmm, no," she said. My mom is brutally honest like that. There was no, "Hmm, okay, sure, maybe it's a little green." Or "Yeah, I can see something, maybe we should have that looked at." Nope. She shut that shit down.

"I'm looking at it, Jen, and it looks normal," she said.

I started screaming and crying, vibrating with fear and frustration. "Then why does it look green to me?"

Were my eyes lying to me? I was sure I was green, but I couldn't prove it. And man did I try. Mostly by raising my voice louder and louder, screaming at my mother to look a little closer, to acknowledge what I knew to be true. Our house was echoey, with superhigh ceilings and, since it was South Florida, wall-to-wall tile. With those acoustics, emotions could not be contained in any one room. My fears were reverberating throughout the whole house.

Everyone knows that ear-piercing screams have a huge leg up on even the most factual or reason-based arguments, but in this case the shrieking didn't work. My mother didn't budge, and we were both exhausted, so we gave up. Fighting was our cardio, and neither of us really liked exercise.

I went up to my room for what we now call self-care but back then was just known as a manicure, and then into my bathroom, where I grabbed a handful of cotton balls, some nail polish remover, a nail file, and a new bottle of Chanel Vamp (most of my money went to high-end nail polish back then). I sat down on the pale peach carpet and started removing the existing polish from my nails. Halfway through, I realized I should light the piña colada–scented candle I had just gotten from Pier 1. Candles, I was certain, were integral to self-care.

As it turns out, mixing manicures and an open flame is not the best idea. Just as the match touched the wick, EVERY SINGLE NAIL ON MY RIGHT HAND caught fire. Yes, fire. This was not me seeing something that wasn't there, like my green skin. This was actual flame fingers, because nail polish remover is highly flammable. I reflexively flapped my hand so fast that the fire was extinguished before any real harm was done, but emotionally I had been triggered, and emotional triggers often come with an intense physiological reaction.

A rush of adrenaline made me feel electrified, like I could turn on a light bulb just by touching it. It seemed like a sign, like the beginning of the end or the start of the beginning. The energy was uncontainable, and I knew I'd have to flail and scream to release it.

I figured fighting could help with that, so I went back downstairs to yell at my parents some more and expose them to my jumbled inner monologue: "I know this whole 'Jen doesn't have green skin' thing is a conspiracy and I hate the way my jeans fit and I don't want to be in this jean-repellant body anymore and what am I even doing here and why didn't you prepare me for life after college and MY FINGERS WERE JUST ON FIRE?!?!"

My mom started screaming back at a comparable volume, while my dad stayed silent—he's the pacifist in the family. "The skin thing isn't a conspiracy," she yelled. "It just isn't real, and if you want your jeans to fit, stop eating so much!"

I was ready for a fight, even if it wasn't a totally coherent one. "You don't even know what it's like to want a chocolate chip cookie, when you know you shouldn't have a chocolate chip cookie, but you still eat the cookie, but you do it over the trash can and you only really eat the chocolate chips and then you throw the rest of the cookie away and then you take some of what you threw away and eat that too! You don't understand that!"

My parents just stared at me blankly, but deep down I'm sure my dad knew what I meant about the cookie.

My body was getting hotter, the fire-fingers adrenaline pumping through my veins and my emotions bubbling faster and faster but still refusing to boil over. In an attempt to let them out, I grabbed an almost-empty bottle of white zinfandel that was on the kitchen counter and slammed it into my forehead.

At least, that's how I remember it. Over the years I have told a version of this story where the wine bottle shattered and my face was covered in glass, cheap white wine, and blood, but in that scenario I certainly would have been rushed to the hospital, which I wasn't. What probably happened was that I grabbed the body of the bottle and bonked myself in the head, not hard enough to shatter the bottle or my skull, but forcefully enough to finally get my parents' full attention and to stop the screaming match that could have gone on for hours.

(This kind of self-inflicted head injury wasn't entirely new for me. My parents say that as a three-year-old, when I didn't get what I wanted, I would drop everything and aggressively bang my head against the floor. I guess I did it in a Bloomingdale's once. We sell ban.do in Bloomingdale's now. Thought you should know.)

The head bonk worked, stunning my parents into silence. The moment created a tiny opening for the super-charged tension to seep out of my body.

I have a permanent snapshot in my mind of my parents standing there, white-faced and wide-eyed in shock. Completely motionless. I knew I had to get out of there, because I still had energy to burn. I grabbed my keys off the counter, hopped in my car, turned up the radio as loud as it could go, and peeled out of the driveway. At first, I felt the overwhelming urge to drive full speed into oncoming traffic, which is a strange urge when you aren't trying to kill yourself. It was also unrealistic, because we lived in a quiet gated community and there wasn't much traffic on the main road. But the adrenaline of the last hour made me feel powerful, until a few minutes into my drive when, like a switch flipping, an odd feeling of complete calm washed over me. The initial intense energy was replaced with a stillness that left me feeling depleted, and so I cried in my car in the middle of the road, feeling scared and embarrassed about what had just happened, but also relieved that whatever I'd been dealing with had finally surfaced.

I sat in that car for what felt like an eternity but was really about twelve minutes, catching my breath and cooling down after the toughest emotional workout of my life. Then, even though I dreaded the coming confrontation with my parents, it was time to go home.

I could hear my parents' muffled voices from outside, but they went silent when I opened the door. Their faces made it very clear they were frightened. My dad looked intimidated, because he knew he was unequipped to deal with whatever was going to come next. But that was okay, because post-emotional-eruption cleanup was my mom's department. In spite of our extremely contentious relationship—which included, but was not limited to, plate slinging, name-calling, and not-so-veiled threats of murder—we were incredibly close. Ours is probably the most intense and spirited relationship I've ever had. And so she did what any mom would do after her child had an incredibly dramatic emotional meltdown—she gave me a hug, told me everything was going to be okay, and sent me to bed with some Tylenol and a warm compress.

I woke up the next day with a big bump on my head and an emotional hangover. I felt numb, but not numb enough to mask the sadness and humiliation. The idea of getting out from under the covers felt insurmountable. It was like I had gone to sleep in my comfy bed on the second floor of our house and woke up in that same comfy bed, but somehow during the night it had been anchored to the bottom of the ocean and I was down there under water. I kind of wanted to stay there forever, hiding from all that had transpired. I was embarrassed, because it was now very clear that there was something really wrong with me. The cat was out of the bag, standing on its two hind legs, wearing a big pink taffeta gown, smoking a cigarette while singing a boisterous rendition of "Fly Me to the Moon."

When I finally went downstairs, my mom was sitting at the dining room table having coffee and writing a list on a legal pad. She told me she'd made an appointment with the doctor, even though I was pretty sure I didn't have a doctor because I hadn't been sick since I'd moved back home. But a doctor felt like the type of professional this situation called for, so I was okay with it. In preparation for the appointment, she asked me to recount any symptoms or otherwise unusual behavior that I'd noticed over the last few days so she could add it to her list.

It was hard to think, it was hard to talk, and, quite frankly, I had no idea what the fuck was going on, but I obliged. "Well, let's see, I accidentally lit my fingers on fire. Sometimes I feel like I can't breathe. My hair feels like it's someone else's, and for the last several days I thought my skin had turned green and no one seemed to notice. My boyfriend of three months, the love of my life, is moving away, so life as I know it is over. My mind won't stop racing, but at the same time all I want to do is lie in bed, and I feel lost and overwhelmed. Oh, and fat."

I looked at my mother, frustrated that I had to spell all this out for her. I wanted her to read my mind or innately know all my internal suffering. I imagine she felt really scared and confused, just as I did, but she didn't show it.

If I had the chance to rewrite that list today with a lot more self-awareness and a heaping dose of emotional intelligence, plus a bunch of plain old information, here is what I would say: "I'm suffering from undiagnosed bipolar disorder, which gives me intense depression with periods of hypomania, but the hypomania is subtle enough that doctors won't notice it and will instead think I just have depression. My mind, caught up in its expectations and fears, is constantly feeding a debilitating anxiety that leaves me, at times, personally and professionally paralyzed. I have ADD, which makes me feel overwhelmed and distracted. Oh, and most of that is just my brain chemistry. Situationally speaking, I am heartbroken because my boyfriend is moving away and I had hinged my identity and all my happiness and my future on him, so I feel empty, and I'm filling that void with food. Lots and lots of food, which has made me gain weight, and so much of my self-worth is tied into how I look, so now I feel horrible about myself and that feeling just makes me want to eat more. I also feel lost, because the real world is intimidating, and I don't feel prepared to be a grown-up. I'm scared of all the responsibility that comes along with it. I don't want to live here with you, but I don't know where to go, and I'm scared to leave. I miss my friends from school. I miss the security of college. I don't know who I am, what I want to do, or where I am going. The world is too big and too scary, and I'll never survive. I feel like a failure. Sometimes I have the urge to do really crazy and erratic things; sometimes I don't want to get out of bed. Sometimes I want to bash my head against the floor to stop the chatter in my mind, the constant narrative reminding me that I am a worthless piece of shit, that I should just give up, that I will never be anything and never do anything. I feel powerless and I am suffering. HELP HELP HELP."

Later that day my mom, her yellow legal pad, and I went to a doctor we had never met so that he could check my blood pressure, hit my knee with that rubber mallet, and assess my debilitating emotional pain all in a matter of thirty minutes. My blood pressure and reflexes were intact. My mom and I took turns listing symptoms and describing the events of the last few days.

"Sounds like you had a nervous breakdown caused by immense stress and some situational depression, and I'm going to give you something to help you feel better," the doctor said as he handed me a prescription for Prozac, an antidepressant that would, over time, exacerbate the bipolar disorder that he missed because he was a general practitioner, not a psychiatrist, and I was a total stranger with whom he spent a half hour. An accurate diagnosis wouldn't come for many more years and would take a lot more work and plenty of psychiatric professionals.

But I took the Prozac, and within just a few days I started to feel better. Calmer. Happier. Less anxious. Less green. *Is this what normal feels like?* I thought to myself. *And if it is, what is the feeling I've been living with for the last twenty-three years?*

It might seem as though having a nervous breakdown and getting a depression diagnosis would have been, I don't know . . . depressing? But what I really felt was both relief and gratitude. I was happy to finally have a name for the feeling that had been haunting me for the past year. I was thrilled to be able to declare I had a mental illness, which is a strange thing to say, but I'd wanted to have something wrong with me for a long time. I think it was to feel special or get attention. Usually I'd wished for an injury or an ailment, like breaking my foot in gymnastics so I could be on crutches and have a cast that everyone could sign, which was a real possibility since I wasn't great at gymnastics. Or maybe to have mononucleosis. Mono was a major deal at the time, and I wanted it so badly. My little brother got it when he was a kid, and my parents told me to stay away from him because it was contagious, but I was so jealous and desperate to be seen that one night I went across the hall into his room and while he slept I leaned over and put my tongue in his mouth. I didn't just pop it in there, I moved it around. Kind of like a tongue swab, because they called mono the kissing disease, and from what I could tell that's what kisses were like. But I didn't get mono, and now I've gone and told thousands of people that I French-kissed my little brother. Cool.

Anyway, this big, weighty depression diagnosis was just the badge I was looking for. I wasn't embarrassed or ashamed. I felt empowered and excited, and I told every-one. (The only person who didn't seem to care was my boyfriend, the one who was leaving. He said depression wasn't real and that I probably just felt sad because we broke up. Almost a decade later, he tracked me down in LA to apologize and admit he was wrong, which he realized when he was diagnosed with depression.)

In the years since, I've had many other depressive and manic episodes, but when I look back over my mental health journey, the wine bottle incident stands out as a truly critical moment. There was no turning back after that. No hiding behind "maybe she has a stomach bug" or "I was just tired." After a lifetime of struggling with mental illness, I have learned that the especially difficult times are precisely when you have the greatest opportunities to learn about yourself, your mental health, your brain, and your body. They are gifts, wrapped in lessons that feel like pain and failure, but I promise if you look at them as gifts, they will eventually reveal themselves as such.

Hallucinating that my skin had turned green might not seem like a gift, but it was the catalyst for my first diagnosis, which would launch my journey toward self-awareness and acceptance and joy.

Of course, the mental health journey is not linear. "Here's a diagnosis! The end!" would make for an awfully short and boring book. Instead, it's a road trip full of detours, construction, flat tires, and maps that are sometimes perfect and other times lead you to horrible and unexpected places. You never arrive at a destination, and sometimes you drive backward for days at full speed without even realizing it. But rather than giving up, you fix the tire, find another route, get a tune-up, and turn your map upside down to see if that makes more sense. Reading maps upside down is a hallmark of my success.

Chapter 2

At the Time, None of Us Knew

When I was a kid, getting me dressed was an exercise in patience.

It was the seventies, so most of my outfits involved a Polly Flinders dress, colored tights, and patent leather Mary Janes.

Wait, I think all of that is cool again.

Anyway, before the clothes could touch my body they had to go through a rigorous color-matching test. The dress had to match the tights *exactly*. I remember my mom trying desperately to reason with me—yes, the blue background of the dress wasn't exactly the same as the lighter blue tights, but the tights actually matched the teeny-tiny blue flowers in the pattern of the dress. I would hold the tights against the dress, putting my face as close to them as possible to assess her argument. This ability to discern very specific shades of blue (or pink, or purple) served me well as a career creative but maybe not as a kindergartener trying to get ready for school. If I'd had Pantone chips during that period of my life, I would have used them as a weapon. (I know this because many years later, after starting ban.do, I did exactly that.)

I should point out that I was cross-eyed during this period of my life, so the sight of me examining my dresses must have been nothing short of magic.

Once the dress-and-tights combo passed the color-matching test, it was on to the fit test. The manner in which the dress and tights and shoes had to fall on my body was very specific. The dress could not be too tight or too loose. Scratchy tags in the neck or sides were grounds for immediate disqualification. The tights had to sit high on my waist, not on my hips—there was about a five-millimeter margin of error. Most important, that fucking seam at the toe of the tights had to be placed precisely at the edge of my toenails. Not under my toes, and definitely not on top of them. The only way for my mom to know for sure if the tights were right was to slip my shoes onto my feet and see whether I smiled or screamed as if I was being dismembered.

Some people might call this behavior obsessive, I call it attention to detail. Later in life I learned it was actually an indication that I'm what's called a "highly sensitive person," but whatever name you choose, it was on full display when I was a flower girl in my aunt and uncle's wedding. Rather than tossing handfuls of petals in the air willy-nilly, without a care for where they landed, I carefully placed the petals one by one in a line to the altar. To me, this just made good sense. I was responsible for ensuring my aunt didn't get lost on her way down the aisle. But in the wedding video, you can see my mom intercept me as I walk toward the altar, trying to convince me that it would be okay to scatter the petals a little bit. I reluctantly agreed, but deep down I knew it could have been better.

Overall, I had a pretty happy and joyful childhood. I was a sunny kid with mostly typical-kid concerns, like "Will I be able to stay awake to see *Saturday Night Live*?" and "Why do I have to do all this homework?" I was very sensitive and very shy, so I wasn't really on the radar at school, and my only extracurricular activity was quitting extracurricular activities. But I was a fun friend and loved to make people laugh once I got to know them.

Some of my closest friends were the kids who lived in my neighborhood. In the time of no cable, internet, or cell phones, who your neighbors were made a big difference, and I definitely got lucky. We found lots of ways to have fun, and since it was Florida, we did most of it with bare feet. We passed the time shaking up two-liter bottles of Coke to create soda fountains on the front yard or pulling the stems out of honeysuckles and eating the honey. We found dead birds and gave them a proper shoebox burial, dug for treasures in our backyards, and played Marco Polo in the pool while enveloped in the scent of gardenias.

On one particularly memorable morning, we were gathered at Debbie's house after a sleepover, eating candy for breakfast and waiting to see if the local radio station would play the song we'd called in to request when Debbie's mom opened the door and stuck her head in. She had a solemn look on her face, and we all fell silent as she scanned the room. When her gaze fell on me, it was clear something was wrong, and that scared me. I've always been empathetic, but often I do more than just understand other people's feelings, I take them on myself. Sometimes

I carry the weight of them like a backpack, other times I casually notice them like a passing puff of colored smoke in the air. In this case, I could feel Debbie's mom's sorrow, and I knew the news wasn't good. "Jenni, your mom needs you at home," she said.

Am I in trouble? Why am I in trouble? Is it because we ate the candy? How does she know we ate candy? These were my first thoughts, which were ridiculous because I was a pretty well-behaved kid, though it's probably the good kids who worry the most. I had no choice but to head home. Slowly, and I mean slow-motion slowly, I got my things together and walked back across the street to my house. I dropped my stuff at the door and walked down the hallway into the living room, running my left hand over the ribbed wallpaper as I went. My mom looked mad, and sad, but she also wore some other foreign expression that made me feel even more uncomfortable.

All I could think was *fingertips, fingertips, fingertips,* over and over, because mine were tingling like crazy. It was as if they wanted to be sure I knew they were there, since most of us don't really think about our fingertips unless they get burned on a hot stove or shriveled in the bath. "Grandpa Bill died," my mom said, in the characteristic blunt tone she has always used when delivering bad news.

It wasn't without sadness or kindness, there was just no beating around the bush.

Grandpa Bill was my father's father and he was a good grandpa. Always game for a forty-five-minute session of Marco Polo in the pool, so clearly a patient man. He was also my first relative to die (the first person I knew to die, period), and his death was out of the blue. That foreign expression on my mother's face? It was shock.

While my mom seemed to be handling the news with a stoic face and measured tone, my dad was not taking it well. This was his dad, after all. He was alone in their bedroom, and I could hear a strange muffled whimpering coming from behind the closed door. It sounded like an injured bear. I had never heard my dad cry and didn't actually know that dads *could* cry. Picturing him curled up in a ball under the covers, sobbing (though I have no idea if that's what was actually happening), was honestly more than I could handle, and I just wanted to go back to my friend's house and eat more candy and forget the whole thing. I did, at some point during those few minutes, start crying. Probably because I was sad, but also because someone was dead and I had definitely seen on TV that the proper reaction was to cry. After a few minutes I felt kind of numb and weird, and so my mom—reluctantly or willingly, I can't remember—let me go back across the street to Debbie's.

I entered my friend's bedroom quietly but also more confidently than I'd ever entered a room up until that point. I don't know if it was because I felt stronger for having just survived a rite of passage, or if my grandfather's death had triggered a mood shift and I was entering into a hypomanic episode, or both. The radio was still on, and the next thing I knew I was standing on the bed, laughing and dancing and flailing my arms and jumping up and down like a contestant on *The Price Is Right*. It felt good, and also like I couldn't stop.

Of course, when your grandpa dies, you shouldn't laugh. It doesn't matter if you're nine, it's just not appropriate, mostly because it's not funny. For a quiet, obedient kid like me, that kind of behavior was completely out of character. I took comfort in doing the right thing and acting appropriately and obeying rules. I listened intently to authority and followed directions. The mere thought of getting in trouble gave me horrible anxiety, though at the time it was just called a stomachache. Obviously, my behavior that morning was uncharacteristic, to say the least.

After a couple of songs, the girls must have thought it was weird to see shy Jenni up on the bed doing the funky chicken, because suddenly my mom was in the room coaxing me off the bed and insisting that I come back home. She didn't yell at me in front of my friends—my mom is not one for a public scene—but as soon as we were home it was clear I had done something wrong.

"Why are you acting that way?" she asked. "This is not a happy day. This is a sad day, and you should be crying, not dancing on beds."

I just stared at her with little huffs of breath coming out of my mouth, either from the dancing or the anxiety, it was unclear. I didn't have an answer for her. I didn't know why I'd gone from feeling really, really sad to feeling really high or why I could hardly breathe. But jumping on the bed is what my brain told my body to do, and at that point in my life, I just followed along. Don't forget, I was nine. It would be a long time before I learned to evaluate my emotions or control my actions during this kind of episode.

I know now that this was an early sign of bipolar disorder—it's always easier to spot the clues with the luxury of hindsight—but at the time none of us knew what was going on, and nine was not an age for introspection, so I just continued being alive without thinking about the time I danced on the bed when my grandpa died, or other times like it, for another twenty years.

I asked my parents about this incident recently. Was it concerning for them? A red flag? Their answer was illuminating. . . . They don't remember it. Outside of myself, these are supposed to be the archivists of my life, or at least of my childhood, and at first I was kind of insulted that they couldn't remember every detail, both major and minor, of my early existence. But then the three of us sat at lunch trying to remember what we had for dinner the night before for, like, six minutes, and we never could figure it out. So there you go.

It's entirely possible that my dad, dealing as he was with the loss of his own father, didn't even know this went down. As for my mom, I'm not sure what she thought. Maybe that I was showing off, or that I was grief-stricken and too young to know how to properly process. In 1980, there was not nearly the awareness of mental health struggles that there is today—and there is still such a long way to go. But it was a bit of a double whammy: I had no idea what was going on with me, because I was a kid and had no self-awareness; and my family couldn't recognize what was going on with me because there was limited mental health awareness in general. Plus, when you're a preteen, issues like depression are especially hard to spot. It's easy to assume any kid who seems down is just angsty or sulking, because being a preteen, and a teenager for that matter, is definitely sulk-worthy. All in all, it was not really an environment that was ripe for emotional growth.

When I really reflect on these memories, it's tempting to feel bad for the young girl dancing on a bed with no real understanding of what's going on inside her head. You might think I'd be sad that no one understood what was going on with me. But these memories don't inspire pity or disappointment. Honestly, as I replay that morning in Debbie's room my first reaction is simply . . . *Huh. Look at that.* In some ways our unawareness was a blessing. It would have been pretty shocking to get diagnosed with bipolar at nine years old, as if being pigeon-toed and needing bifocals wasn't enough. Sometimes I wonder if my family could have done a better job of reading the signs, but there's so much subtlety in diagnosing mental illness. If I had failed out of school or refused to get out of bed for long periods of time, we may have noticed something sooner, but I was generally happy and high-functioning, so we just powered through until the signs got too big to ignore. So I don't feel sorry for my nine-year-old self, but boy do I empathize with her.

Of course, I wasn't always so understanding. When I was twenty-nine, shortly after being diagnosed with ADD, I came home to visit my parents. By then I lived in LA, but the Florida sun is a special sun, and I like to make it back at least a couple of times a year. While rifling through old photos, I came across a collection of my report cards. We can't find my goddamn birth certificate but my report cards? Saved for posterity, every last one of them, elementary school all the way through college.

I found the comments from my teachers intriguing to say the least. Shall I treat you to a sampling?

"Jenni is a sweet girl, well liked, but doesn't pay attention in class."

"Jenni seems very tired a lot."

"I can see that Jenni is extremely gifted but she does not complete assignments."

"Jenni is so well behaved, but is distracted."

After reading a handful of these, I did what any self-respecting adult visiting her parents would do and called for my mom at the top of my lungs. "Moooooooooom! Come here right now!" I shouted this down the stairs, because when civilized people are in the comfort of their childhood homes, they do stuff like unbuttoning their pants when they are full and screaming from far distances.

My mom came up the stairs. A little slowly for my liking, but whatever.

"Do you ever look back at these report cards—"

"No, honey, I don't think I do."

"No, I wasn't done," I said. "Do you ever look back at these report cards and wonder how you could have missed the fact that I had ADD?"

And then I proceeded to read each and every comment aloud to her, in that condescending way daughters default to when they're with their mothers, even when they are grown adults. "What do you have to say for yourself?!" I said. "The evidence is right in front of us!"

"I'm sorry," she said. "I missed it. I was doing my best. It's easier to see these things in retrospect."

And she was right. It really, really is.

Chapter 3

I Got It from My Parents

When I was a teenager, my mom and I sounded exactly the same. I would answer our landline phone and whoever was calling would think I was her.

"Saerina?" they'd ask.

"No, it's Jenni, I'll get her for you," I'd say. After a while I realized it would be way more fun if I said, "Yes, it's me." And man was it ever! If you have the chance to impersonate your mom on the phone and say stuff like, "Remember the last time we smoked pot?" or "Our kids are so annoying, right?" I highly recommend you do it. The responses make for great conversation around the Thanksgiving table.

The truth is, I secretly loved that I could pass for my mom. I took it as a sign that I was worthy of her approval. Sometimes I got that. Many times I didn't.

My mother was not like the other moms in Boca Raton, who placed a lot of importance on designer handbags and perfectly styled hair. While the other kids were listening to Top 40 radio on the ride home from school, my mom would suggest we listen to the audiobook of Wayne Dyer's *The Sky's the Limit*. She was open to spirituality and self-improvement long before it was trendy, and, even today, her bookshelf (not unlike my own) is brimming with titles like *The Power of Now* by Eckhart Tolle, *Radical Acceptance* by Tara Brach, and *The Four Agreements* by Don Miguel Ruiz. Her style is original. She can mix and match with the best of them—pattern on pattern, unexpected color combinations, current styles paired with vintage. When I was growing up she was shy and sweet, and, as a girl, I modeled my shyness and sweetness after her. But there's a complexity beyond her kind exterior. She's thoughtful and introspective and creative, and in an increasingly performative social media world, she has nothing to prove. (This is why you won't catch a glimpse of her on my Instagram. My dad, Dr. Jamie, is a whole other story. He loves the camera, and the camera loves him.) When she's not doing the *New York Times* crossword, my mom is painting or writing poems—she's written hundreds and hundreds of poems—and when I was a kid we shopped and watched TV together and I would help her make necklaces for the small jewelry-design business she used to run out of our home.

My mother has been my rock in some very dark times. I owe her a huge debt of gratitude, but for a long time my attitude was guided by far less positive emotions. Namely anger and resentment. After all, what daughter doesn't have a mental archive of every time her mother has wronged her? Who hasn't been shaped by well-intentioned but poorly delivered remarks that were a blip for the mom who uttered them but daggers to the heart for those of us on the receiving end? I learned recently that it takes five positive comments to equal the impact of one negative one, and I believe it. This ratio did no favors for my relationship with my mom in my teen years—I'm certain she said nice things, she assures me she did, but I couldn't tell you what they were.

Which may explain why I was mad at her from the time I was twelve until I was thirty-five.

Some of my anger was warranted, although much of

it was not. Ours was—and is—a complex relationship, as most mother-daughter bonds are.

My mom was twenty-three when she had me. It was the early seventies, when there was not nearly the same emotional awareness around parenting that there is today. She was a first-time mom and the child of Holocaust survivors who immigrated to America shortly after she was born. My grandfather was married with three kids before he met my grandma. His first wife and children were killed in a concentration camp while he worked in a forced labor camp. My grandmother survived Auschwitz and met my grandfather at a soup kitchen she ran in Budapest after the war. They survived the unimaginable, and I'm not a psychologist (yet), but I think it's safe to assume they both had some form of PTSD. After seeing that much horror, I imagine my grandparents were always on guard, bracing for the worst, or at the very least keeping a safe distance from the people dearest to them.

My mom says that her father was always very guarded and protective of his emotions, but I actually remember him as a great grandpa. Sweet and smiling, with the kindest eyes. He was always joking around, and I felt really loved by him, though I understand that grandparenting is basically parenting without any of the responsibility, so it was probably easier for him to loosen up by then. My grandma was a tough woman, and my mom says she wasn't very maternal. But she was incredibly resilient and also quite honest—Jewish guilt oozed from her pores. Once, when she came to stay with us for a visit, I overheard her ranting about the accommodations to my mother and then, mid-argument, shift to Yiddish. She only broke out the Yiddish when she had something disparaging to say, and I saw the look on my mother's face, so I knew whatever she said, it wasn't good.

"What did she say?" I asked my mom.

"She said it was better in Auschwitz," my mom responded, sounding defeated but not surprised.

I was an insecure teenager. I felt unseen and unheard, like the real me was trapped inside and couldn't get out. Also, my boobs were too small and my butt was too big, and while I had cute girl-next-door looks I knew I was not a showstopper.

My friend Angie, she was a showstopper. And not just because of her looks, though with her big doe eyes and long tan legs she was indeed beautiful. Her personality— her essence, really—was magnetic. She was confident, fun, likable, and always laughing. People gravitated to her whenever she entered a room. Me, not so much. I was more of a like-her-once-you-get-to-know-her type, but in order to know her you'd have to notice her. The difference between us felt, at least to me, pretty glaring. One night, I must have been confiding in my mom about feeling insufficient and constantly in Angie's shadow, because she sat me down and looked me right in the eyes.

"Jenni, Angie is a diamond," my mom said. "She sparkles. People are attracted to her because she's so shiny and bright. And you? Well, you're a pearl. Still beautiful, but in a quieter way. You may not always get noticed, but that's okay. You're a classic."

I was gutted.

I was sixteen and it was the eighties. Everyone wanted to be bold and bright and truly, truly, truly outrageous like Jem (and the Holograms). I couldn't understand the nuance of being subtly beautiful or the value in being a classic. Stuffy old ladies wore pearls. I wanted to be popular, like, NOW. Desired. Sparkly. Seen. I wanted to be a diamond.

The thing is, my mom was right. I know that now. (She almost always is.) I was not the girl who inspired guys to walk across a crowded room and compliment their beauty—I've never been that girl. (I cried when I first wrote that sentence, because I would love to know what it feels like to sparkle in that way. I've never experienced it, though I've often seen it firsthand—every single one of my best friends has been a diamond.) Still, to hear it confirmed by the one person whose approval I sought the most was devastating, and sometimes I wonder if my tendency to feel invisible around men and my intense insecurity around dating is a response to this one silly comment.

To be fair, my mom thought calling me a pearl was a compliment. That it was the preferable state, because diamonds fade. And if she said it today, I might even take it that way. I think pearls are having a comeback.

But at sixteen? No.

I hated that I didn't look perfect, which of course was not even a real thing, but I obsessed over my appearance and fixated on the most nitpicky problems because I had an idea that if I looked a certain way, it would make me enough. At one point in college I became hung up on my profile. I must have seen a picture of it that I didn't like. It dominated my thoughts, which left very little brain space to, you know, learn and study. I was particularly fixated on my teeth. They jutted out of my mouth at an angle that was not anything I'd seen on movie stars or in magazines, which meant they were a problem. I'd already had braces, but my mom encouraged me to go to the orthodontist to see what he thought. She was trying to alleviate my suffering so I could feel better and focus on school. So I went to the orthodontist, and he assured me that it wasn't so bad and there wasn't anything that could be done about it anyway. Bummed, I gave my mom the news.

"Honey, you should get a second opinion," she said. "The more I think about it, the more I realize it really is an unattractive overbite."

Ouuuuuuuuch.

I know now that she wasn't trying to hurt me. This was, again, her attempt at honesty and support. I still have to remind her that sometimes, Mom, sometimes honesty is not the best policy, especially when talking about someone's teeth. But I think she thought it was better I hear it from her than from somebody else.

My teeth still do the thing, but somewhere around the age of forty-three I decided it was cute and not stupid. There's a real beauty, and freedom, in acceptance.

I love my mom. Without her I would not have my sensitivity or creativity, my emotional intelligence or open-mindedness or self-awareness. She encouraged my fashion sense and vulnerability and my strong proclivity for rom-coms starring Meg Ryan. And my originality.

"Dare to be different, Jenni," she always told me, and I thought that sounded scary, but she must have said it enough for it to stick, because I never conformed to what everyone else was doing. When collecting stickers was all the rage, my friends would flock to the sticker place in the mall while I'd make my parents drive me to Home Depot to get translucent butterfly decals for sliding glass doors, or garage sale price tag stickers. When tube tops were popular, I chose button-up oxfords. When everyone was straightening their hair, I got a perm—which was a disaster because I had bangs, and if you have ever permed your bangs, you know what I mean.

But still, we fought. A lot. My mom was all about honesty and directness, no matter the occasion, and her intention was always to encourage and protect me, to prepare me for the scrutiny of the harsh outside world and even harsher teenage girls. But for a highly sensitive, insecure daughter who craved constant approval and unconditional love, it was a bad match, and my immediate reaction to my mother's "just being honest" comments varied depending on the day. Sometimes they made me want to shrivel up and disappear, sometimes they made me want to do anything and everything to be better, and sometimes they made me want to go on a killing spree, and by *spree* I mean kill only her, but kill her a million times.

There is one reason my mom and I didn't murder each other, and that reason was my dad. He brought a lighthearted humor that diffused the tension between the two women in his life. For better or for worse, he's a true people pleaser, so he did everything he could to keep both of us happy. He was the peacekeeper in the middle of a hormonal war zone. For a little while in high school, I worked reception in his office, and since my mother was the office manager, she was essentially my boss. You can imagine how well that went. But one day, after she and I had been arguing about my lack of follow-through on office responsibilities and her need to call me out on that, as any respectable Boss Mom would, my dad called me back into his office.

"Uh, Jenni, can I see you for a moment? I lost something in here."

In between patients, he had taken some of those wooden-handled cotton swabs that all doctors seem to have in their office and stuck them securely into his nose and ears. The moment he heard me open the door he swiveled around on his little wheely stool to reveal his look, and in a very serious tone asked, "Have you seen the Q-tips?"

The tension immediately left my body, and I tried not to laugh, because I was at the age where I still acted like he wasn't funny, just an embarrassment.

His goofy attempts to lighten the mood always worked, and I've learned to employ the same tactics when I'm around tension, whether in the office or between friends. Plus, as anyone who has seen my dad on Instagram knows (he's @drjamie14, breakout star of my Stories), he's wacky and good-natured and doesn't take himself too seriously. He's really a breath of fresh air.

I recently interviewed my parents for an episode of my podcast, and I asked them what they didn't like about me. My mom sat quietly, I imagine alphabetizing her list, while my dad looked at me and said, "Nothing." Nothing? Oh, come on, there's got to be something. Meanwhile I could see my mom chomping at the bit just waiting to be called on. "Nothing," he repeated. "I think you're perfect." And, honestly, I can feel that emanating off him when we're together. If I had two parents like that, I'd probably be some kind of spoiled self-important monster. But the balance of my dad's genuine approval and my mom's judgment made me kind of cool. Today my dad is one of my best buds. I talk to him on the phone every day, and one of the things I love most about those conversations is that he's so consistent. With my dad, 99 percent of the time you know what you're going to get, and, as someone with generalized anxiety, I find a lot of comfort in that.

My parents, although very cool, were in many ways stereotypical neurotic Jewish parents, constantly worrying for my safety. Everything from "Make sure to bring a coat" to, when I was elected sorority president, "That seems like a lot of work, will you be able to handle it?" When my friends started to get their licenses, it was a nonstarter. "If you get in a car with an inexperienced driver, you might die," they said.

And I thought about dying a lot. In fact, by the time I was in college, I developed pretty severe travel anxiety. It stuck with me for most of my adult life but first manifested as a full-on panic attack just before I was supposed to board an airplane back to school. It was the end of my Thanksgiving break, and as my parents and I were walking through the airport, somewhere between security and the store where you buy Kit Kats and *People* magazine, a strange sensation came over me. (This was the early nineties, back when you could keep your shoes, belts, glasses, jewelry, and cardigans on and you didn't even need to be a ticketed passenger to accompany someone to the gate or greet them at the gate or even propose to them at the gate just as they stepped off the plane. Now it's just sad and lonely and no one asks anyone to marry them at the gate anymore.) My legs and fingertips felt tingly, like they do after drinking a glass of champagne. My chest felt really tight, as if some jerk had parked their Ford F-150 on my sternum. And I knew, with more conviction than I have ever known anything, that I was absolutely, without a doubt, going to die on that plane. I didn't know *how* the plane would go down, but I was sure it would be a slow-motion, horrifying death. So I did what anyone walking to a certain death would do. I fell into the closest chair, cried, hyperventilated, and refused to take another step closer to that ill-fated aluminum coffin. For some reason my parents' worry for my life didn't apply to air travel (anxiety works in mysterious ways), so after some back-and-forth—"You're *not* going to die!" "I *am* going to die!" "You're *not* going to die!"—they surrendered and brought me home, and I ended up getting a ride back to school with a friend.

P.S. My parents have no recollection of this event. Given what we saw in the last chapter, is anyone surprised?

I also worried about being kidnapped. And being incapable and overwhelmed. And being cold—I always worry about being cold. And I have a setting that will take all that worry and give it a physiological response in the form of an anxiety attack. It's quite a cocktail.

I'm not assigning fault for anything in my life—we get what we get, and we don't get upset—but of course my parents contributed to who I am, through both nature and nurture. Case in point, my mom and dad both have evidence of mental health issues in their families. This was my inheritance. (Along with my olive-toned skin and thick gorgeous hair, thankyouverymuch.) And although mental illness was never a topic of conversation with my dad, it absolutely was with my mom. She herself struggled with mental health issues for most of her adult life, and as a result, she worked painstakingly to help me feel better physically, emotionally, and mentally. She became my emotional point person, eventually encouraging me to monitor my moods so that we could try to combat depressive or hypomanic episodes before my mental health got away from me.

It can be easy, while looking back on our lives and our shortcomings and our pain, to home in on our parents and point the finger. Sometimes the middle finger, sometimes just the normal pointer finger. But these days I find myself incredibly grateful for the things I inherited. My closest friends, and even the people who know me only from Instagram, always comment on my humor, my sense of fashion, and my willingness to self-reflect without shame or self-editing. I have my parents to thank for all of it. My ability to broach difficult topics with lightheartedness is partly what earned me the opportunity to host a podcast and write this book. It's not always easy to look at your parents without judgment and accept all your inherited traits, good and bad, but you have to understand where you come from to truly understand who you are—and only then can you start figuring out who you want to be.

Chapter 4

This Winding Road

A few weeks after my nervous breakdown (you remember, the green-skin, fire-fingers, wine-bottle one?), I felt stuck. I wanted to move to New York City. I was born there, both my parents grew up there, and it just seemed like a really exciting place to figure out the rest of my life.

My dad didn't really see it that way. It was too dangerous, he said. Too dangerous and too cold. The dreaded c-word.

I'm not sure about the danger (though it was 1995, and the New York City crime rate was much higher than it is today), but my dad was definitely right about the cold.

When I was three, our family lived in Southern California while my dad did his podiatry residency at Edwards Air Force Base, so he suggested I move to San Diego instead. (I knew my dad was going to finance this next adventure, so he got a lot of input.) And so I moved across the country without a job, a place to live, or any idea of what I was going to do or who I was going to be.

When I arrived in San Diego I was exhilarated, hopeful, and free. I spent the first couple of weeks fantasizing about my new life while living in a teeny-tiny hotel room where no matter how I was lying in bed, my feet could always touch two walls. Eventually, I found the cutest studio apartment in an old historic building near Balboa Park called the Barcelona. It had one of those elevators with an iron gate you have to close, which was the coolest thing I had ever seen. My predictably neurotic parents were convinced it was a death trap, and I'm sure I thought about plunging to my untimely end every time I got in, but my desire for a cool living space won out over my anxiety . . . this time.

I had no career plan, or even any real career qualifications. In college, unlike my friends who took classes in the areas that would become their livelihoods, I bounced around from major to major. Initially I had my eyes on business, not because I actually wanted to pursue it but because all the hot guys at FSU were business majors. Then, because I was a huge sports fan—not playing, just watching—I switched to sport management. Also, again, hot guys. Then I decided to become a writer, but I didn't get into the writers' program (ha ha, look at me now) so instead I opted for a degree in English lit. I hated it, but a year in I found out that with a philosophy minor and a couple of years of Latin, it could be considered prelaw. This felt like a very respectable choice, and I was already pretty good at arguing and convincing people of my point of view. Basically I could mind-meld people. Still can.

About a semester before graduation, I decided I didn't want to be a lawyer either. I left college without any idea of what I would do with my life, but two years later, in San Diego, I discovered a love for all things vintage and briefly ran a small antiques and faux-finishing business called Vincent's Ear and Other Lost Treasures. (I was incredibly proud of that name.) It was essentially a stall smack-dab in the middle of a large antiques mall, next to homogenous booths full of Victorian cookware and sports memorabilia. Most days I would hang there, covered in a combination of paint and Mod Podge, smiling among the color and chaos of decoupaged tables, brightly painted chairs, and tchotchkes as far as the eye could see. I'd happily talk to the passersby, connecting with them over the memories the items in my booth inspired. This was in the height of the shabby-chic trend, so I'd buy a $5 thrift store chair, paint and sand it to look kind of aged, and resell it for $40—which I now know is an excellent profit margin. But even though I sold a fair bit of stuff, I bought more than I could sell and more than I could afford, and for every item sold, I gave away two for free—which I now know is a horrible profit margin. (It wasn't that different from the early days of ban.do, when our trade-show booth always looked different and eventually I was forbidden from taking orders because I could be talked into giving a discount to even the smallest order.)

Unsurprisingly, Vincent's Ear didn't last long. Still, it was my first business, and it laid down roots for my later, successful creative endeavors, so while it felt like a miss at the time, it turned out to be an integral part of my career. I still like to give stuff away for free, but now I have a CEO and CFO to protect me from myself and protect the business from me.

I moved to Los Angeles exactly one year after I arrived in San Diego. I was floundering and had become convinced that LA could be a catalyst for big change in my life. It was so different from San Diego, which was pristine but had a very calm, almost nonexistent energy. San Diego felt a lot like South Florida, which made it a great transition city, but LA was electric. It felt alive and welcoming, and, on some level, I knew I could plug into that energy and make something of my life. Plus moving meant that I could leave all my failures behind, which is a coping method I had already used several times in my life.

Once I got to LA, I decided to become an actress, because surely it would be easy to get acting work in Hollywood with zero training and very little self-confidence, right? Lucky for me, the notion of being a struggling actress was more appealing than actually acting, so I did what most struggling actresses do and got a part-time, low-paying job at the Pottery Barn in the Beverly Center mall, and enrolled in night classes at ABC Bartending School. I was first in my class, because I am an incredibly fast learner. I could make a sex on the beach in under a minute, and I actually found mixology to be pretty fun, though I never did end up tending bar, not even for a night.

In addition to Pottery Barn and bartending school, I signed up to be a film and TV extra as a way to break into the industry. I knew that as an extra I would be in the background—having a drink at the bar, riding the subway, sitting in class with the main characters—but I didn't know it meant I'd be at the bottom of the on-set food chain, the group of us corralled into tiny rooms with no food or water for what felt like hours at a time. When I did get on set, I was a no one. I felt alternatively invisible or like a prop instead of a person.

The message to the extras was always the same: "You are less than." We were a group without rights, always sitting in a room feeling like production forgot about us, and when they remembered us they almost exclusively called each of us "Hey you."

Despite my disdain for the way I was treated on set, I managed to get on TV a lot, and I was easy to spot, due to a platinum-blond pixie cut inspired by the character of Jane on the popular TV drama *Melrose Place.* On any given night I could be spotted walking through a scene on shows like *Boy Meets World, Party of Five,* or *Sabrina the Teenage Witch.* My friends and family thought I was famous. I didn't dispute that or tell them about the tiny room with no food, but I did tell them about the time I met Jason Priestly on the set of *Beverly Hills, 90210.*

I took a couple of film- and commercial-acting classes, and I even auditioned for a national TV ad once. I had to pretend to be an attendant at a gas station and run around four empty folding chairs (the "car"), miming things like taking the driver's credit card, pumping gas, and, for some reason, bringing the driver a completely cooked turkey on a platter.

To no one's surprise, I didn't get the job, and embarrassed by the rejection, I decided acting wasn't for me. But while it didn't connect with me as a career, the professional hierarchy of show business and the disparate treatment of the "talent" versus the "help," always stuck with me.

And so it was back to the drawing board, this time feeling lost and ashamed, sentiments that were additionally fueled by my depression. By that point, many of my friends from college had opted for a secure and traditional adulthood, settling down and taking jobs as accountants, teachers, and sales reps. They bought houses, started families, worked forty hours a week, and then, on the weekends, they intentionally had fun, playing in softball leagues or going to concerts. It seemed that many of them lived their passions outside of their jobs, which is not to say they weren't happy in their careers but that they were able to mentally and emotionally separate in a way that I never could, even when I didn't actually have a career. The concept of having a job that paid the bills and then pursuing your interests on nights and weekends seemed completely absurd to me. I wanted to be able to say "I'm a *this*" or "I'm a *that*" even though I had no idea who I was, or what "this" or "that" could possibly be. I wanted a career that was fun, not just a paycheck, and one that felt special and unique, so that when people heard what I did, they immediately thought I was special and unique too.

By this time I was in therapy (more on that shortly), and my therapist made it a priority to help me figure out what I wanted to do. Plus, a steady income, even if it was minimum wage, would give me more self-esteem, she said.

Trying to figure out my passions was like digging for treasure, and I have always loved digging for treasure. Over one summer in the early eighties my friend and I basically dug up her whole yard in search of buried treasure. What we found instead was a disgusting amount of worms, a faded lighter from 7-Eleven, and half an old plastic Easter egg, but no treasure.

My therapist and I had better luck, and after I mentioned that I was intrigued by the people behind the scenes when I was an extra, she encouraged me to pursue entry-level work in the art departments of film studios. The art department is the group that gives a film its visual identity, and while I landed a number of interviews, it took a while before any of them led to a job offer. I imagine they could sense that my heart wasn't really in it. Now that I'm on the hiring side of things I know how easy it is to recognize who wants the job and who isn't totally sold. Passion for the company and the job itself, if palpable, is almost always enough for a second interview at ban.do. We have tried hiring people who were less passionate but highly qualified, and it has failed miserably.

I did eventually get a job in a production company art department, and I enjoyed how fast-paced and collaborative the work was. I didn't stick with it for long, because I noticed that the women who had been doing it for decades all looked really tired and listless and I didn't want that for myself, but I was interested in similarly team-oriented work.

For the next few years I bounced around from one seemingly meaningless job to the next—I did some copywriting for a small ad agency, where I got to write some very riveting descriptions of how DSL is faster than cable internet, and I taught art to ten-year-olds, though honestly I wasn't much better than they were. I spent my spare time (of which I had a fair bit) pursuing creative interests in an effort to uncover my passions. I took a bunch of photography classes and also a sewing class, for which I sacrificed my red velvet flocked vintage kitchen curtains in order to make a pair of pants that ended up having only one leg hole. I kept them for five years; I have a hard time letting things go.

In and among all this professional exploration, I was still struggling with my mental health, so it was hard for me to be consistent about pursuing or maintaining jobs. I could be struck down at any time with a bout of depression that would last weeks if not months and quickly derail any professional progress I had made. Because of this, I found myself gravitating to work that was less of a long-term commitment and once again found myself signing up to be a temp. I know, I know, I thought I hated temp work, but, like some of the other jobs I dipped my toes into, this one turned out to have immense value. I didn't realize it at the time, because it was low-level assistant work, but looking back I was gaining useful life skills almost daily. Plus, I was introduced to one of my first mentors, a woman named Dodd. You never know when or from where you'll find a role model, and I've found it can happen in some pretty unexpected places and at some pretty unexpected times.

Dodd had a one-woman efficiency-consulting business, something I've found most businesses need. She essentially evaluated how a business operated and then worked to make it more economical in both a time and revenue sense. She was tall, blond, and beautiful, but she didn't flaunt it. She looked like Daryl Hannah and had a cool, raspy voice and only said fuck when she really needed to (a major life lesson). Despite the fact that she worked alone in her office, she almost always wore a really nice business suit to work. She was in her late thirties, single, and while she was very honest about her emotions and shortcomings, she was still very strong and easy to respect. She needed some help around her office, and we hit it off immediately. I didn't entirely understand what she did, but I knew I admired her and, because of that, within hours of knowing her she became someone I desperately wanted to please. At the end of the first day she asked me to come back again the next day, and at the end of the second day she called the temp agency that had placed me, paid them a finder's fee, and hired me on as her assistant.

Dodd taught me a lot of "adult skills" that maybe I should have already known, while also paying me. I kept track of all her bills and made sure the checks were mailed on time and recorded in the company bookkeeping program. I did her grocery shopping, learning the importance of the simple yet too-often-avoided shopping list—we all think we can do it without one, but we never truly can. I organized paperwork, booked travel, maintained her office, even decorated her Christmas tree, which for a nice Jewish girl from Boca Raton was a real thrill. If there was a problem with the plumbing, I called a plumber, and if her car was making a funny noise, I took it into a mechanic. It all sounds simple, but I really hadn't learned most of these skills because they aren't taught on *Law & Order*—canvas a crime scene, yes, base-level adulting, no. You learn by doing, and I did, so I learned.

I should add that plenty of these tasks, like calling the plumber or organizing bills, made me anxious and still do. But I did them anyway, because they were my job. It turned out that once I was working for someone I respected, I had a pretty stellar work ethic.

The other great thing about this job was that Dodd was an all-around amazing human. She was very straightforward and honest, even about very private things in her life. She was interested in personal growth, always reading books and going to seminars (some of which she would bring me along for), and she was very conscious of her health. Not in an impossibly strict diet or excessive workout kind of way, she just had an awareness of the line between healthy and unhealthy habits and always tried to land on the right side of that. Being the kind of person who looks after yourself in this way really sets you up to care for others in a similar fashion, and Dodd always looked after me. She was kind and patient and showed a lot of compassion about my mental health issues. Because I felt comfortable with Dodd I was always open with her about my struggles—which were still pretty significant at the time—even though that probably wasn't "professional." Having not spent much prolonged time in any professional relationships, I didn't know any better. I felt safe. Plus, I've never been able to keep that sort of personal information to myself, so really I felt safe telling anyone who would listen. Later, when I had assistants and eventually a team of people working for me, I would come to realize how valuable my experience with Dodd was. I learned from her that it's possible, and even preferable, to be both authoritative and compassionate, and to mix business relationships with personal ones.

I used to think the significance of my work with Dodd was that it kept me humble, because I also cleaned her toilets, and it was cool to say that one of my early jobs was cleaning toilets. But humility, although a valuable takeaway, was not the most important one. The biggie was this understanding of how positions of authority are actually opportunities to shape and mentor the people who work for you, not just tell them what to do. Dodd operated with a ton of kindness and patience, and she was the first of a handful of bosses who illustrated for me a way to be an adult and a boss that was different from what I'd seen in books or movies, or even in the short-lived jobs I'd had thus far. Other bosses along the way were similarly generous, but it all started with Dodd, so she made a huge impression. She leaned in to my development as part of her job and was always teaching as we went. I never once heard her mutter, "Just figure it out, it's your job." Everything was "ours."

On top of all that, she took a chance on someone with a skill set that was a bit lacking for the job requirements, and I've never forgotten that. In the early days of ban.do, I did the same. If I liked someone and felt like they were connected to the work, I'd happily help them learn the practical skills of the job.

I worked for Dodd part-time for many years while I pursued other more-long-term career possibilities. Along the way I discovered prop styling, which was basically selecting, prepping, and placing all the props (other than humans) in a photo shoot in order to create an overall aesthetic or set a scene—whatever vibe the photographer and client are going for. Think *Real Simple* covers, Nordstrom catalogs, and ads for really nice bed linens. It seemed like fun and potentially something I could be good at, so I started emailing stylists and offering to work for free. I know that's not a viable option for everyone, but if you can swing it, it's a great way to get a foot in the door because you get exposure and you learn a lot and there's far less pressure when you're not getting paid. One of the stylists I emailed turned out to be a food stylist, tasked with making prop food look delicious in photos. She needed some help the next day, so I signed on to help her make a partially raw turkey look oven-baked. Over the next few years, I assisted one food stylist and one prop stylist, learning as much as I could, working on my portfolio and doing test shoots with photographers' assistants until I eventually signed with an agent so I could go out on my own.

I loved styling. It called on my creativity and natural problem-solving abilities. The time commitments were short—usually a job was just a couple of days or a week at most—so there was no time to get sick of it and quit, and I got to meet a lot of interesting people. One time I was hired for a Dairy Queen commercial with the requirement that I make them fake soft-serve ice cream for the shoot. I had no idea how to do that, but I said yes and then figured it out. (It involved a lot of trial and error and, strangely, cake frosting.) After surviving several more yeses to things

I had no idea how to do, I started to build some real confidence in my work.

I worked as a stylist for many more years, and I was incredibly fueled and fulfilled by it. Finally, after all these years of searching, I found a career that I loved! One that saw me gain financial independence, a personal aesthetic, and professional confidence. I experienced, firsthand, what it felt like to plug into my passion. That personal and professional growth blossomed into new aspirations and a desire to expand beyond just styling. Eventually, the challenge of the work wore off. I was still having fun, but it felt monotonous, and I wasn't waking up as excited as I once was. This is important to note about your own work. Just because you find a career that you love doesn't mean you are tethered to it for life, even if you love your coworkers and make a lot of money. My path continued (and continues) to wind in unexpected ways, but only because I let it.

I moved onward and upward and started doing less styling and more art direction (now I guided a stylist through executing my vision) and developed a deep interest in photography, which started when I first got my hands on a Polaroid camera at age ten and slowly and quietly grew so big that there was no denying it was there. I was taking pictures all the time. At work, at home, on the weekends—that's always a good indication of a true passion. I worked my way into commercial photography based on all the connections I had made over the years, and because, well, I was actually pretty good at it. I still took styling and art-directing jobs to stay busy and earn money, and I started a blog about my Polaroid photography (mypolaroidblog.blogspot.com—it's still live!), and then another blog about my love of food and food photography, because having one blog would have been too simple. It turned out later that those blogs connected me with a huge network of people that would end up giving me the support to help launch and grow ban.do. When your intuition guides you to do something, don't wonder why. Just do it and eventually you'll find out.

I had to try out all those different and seemingly random jobs in order to end up in the right place. And I learned something from each job that I eventually incorporated into my career, whether it was how to inspire collaboration, or how *not* to treat an employee. They all contributed to the creative professional that I eventually became. So while I'm not trying to use this book to force my résumé on you (unless you'd like to offer me the job of twerker in chief, in which case, call me), I do think it's important to understand that my career did not follow a straight line, and that even the most unexpected jobs taught me lessons that would eventually affect the way I run my business. If there's one thing I've learned as a founder and entrepreneur, it's that everyone loves an origin story, and mine was more like an origin journey.

This winding road is not unlike the road to mental health. You don't just get a diagnosis and then get cured. Your body changes, your brain changes, you need to do the work and the exploration and go through the trial and error. It's a lifelong process, and I think of careers in that same way.

Sometimes I find myself on panels or doing Q and As in front of big crowds and inevitably some young audience member will ask how I got to where I am today, or what they should be doing now to have a career like mine in ten years. My answer is always that there is no one way. I didn't plan to start a company or sell a company or be a chief creative officer. I didn't study business, and my résumé certainly didn't reflect anything that would indicate that I was qualified or prepared to be a business person, and yet I did it. I am proof that a career path doesn't have to be linear—that you don't have to decide at ten, twenty, thirty, or even forty what your exact path is going to be, and you may have many iterations of a career throughout your life. I'm also proof that if you know the job you want, and you can't find it, you can create it. Remember, no one was the chief creative officer of ban.do before I was.

Listen, there's nothing wrong with having a plan, or knowing what you want to do and pursuing that. Plans are fucking awesome, especially if you can have a healthy relationship with your plan so that if it isn't working you aren't blindly tethered to it but can identify the problem and adjust. But there are other approaches too, and it's okay to feel lost. I was. I know now that I was being led by something, it just wasn't something I could articulate. What I was doing was following my gut and letting the universe show me the way. Because I didn't know what I wanted to be when I grew up until I actually grew up. Sometimes I'm *still* not entirely sure.

Chapter 5

"Can I Call You Mom?" and Other Things I Said to My Therapist

My journey to therapy, and ultimately an accurate diagnosis, started as most journeys of this type do: with a really hot guy. I was a twenty-four-year-old in Los Angeles who still didn't have the emotional equipment to be a functioning adult, so I did what came naturally—I spent money I didn't have on things I didn't need, watched a lot of TV, and barhopped five nights a week. I watched enough *Oprah* at the time to know she might not approve of these decisions, but I was twenty-four, and knowing better didn't always mean doing better. One night, I hopped into an Irish pub on Fairfax called Molly Malone's, and that's where I first saw Jay Gibson.

Jay was the first boyfriend I had in LA, and he was the perfect distraction from the work I should have been doing on my own emotional growth. He was thirty-two, so I thought he was a grown-up, which he sort of was, and sort of wasn't. Not only was he in one of the coolest bands in town, and friends with *Friends* (like the actual cast of *Friends*; we once went on a double date with Jennifer Aniston and her boyfriend Tate Donovan—NBD), he was also fucking hot. The kind of hot that when you point him out to your friends and say "That's the guy I want to date," they spit out their drinks and laugh directly in your face. In the case of my friends, literally.

So you can imagine my glee when Jay Gibson asked ME out. I had given him my phone number—well, I'd put my phone number on his band's mailing list with a little heart by my name because when you're twenty-four you don't think it's pathetic to put a heart next to your name to get a guy's attention. I thought nothing of it. Well, actually, my phone number on that piece of paper and Jay seeing it and calling me was all I could think about.

A few weeks later, my roommates and I were checking our communal answering machine, and between a message from Kristen's mom and a notification that Nicole's dry cleaning was ready, Jay fucking Gibson left a brief message asking me out on a date. My heart was beating so hard and my excitement was so overwhelming that I could barely hear what he said. I thought I was going to lift off into space and explode into a thousand pieces, but instead of losing my cool, I slowly and calmly cocked my head to one side, smiled at my dumbfounded roommates, and said with a giant smile, "I told you so."

The next weekend, Jay and I went out for sushi and a ride on the Santa Monica Pier Ferris wheel. Dinner was great, and he laughed at all my jokes—my humor has always been what attracts or repels a guy, depending on the guy. It makes me appear strong and confident, even when I'm feeling anything but. After the laughs and the raw fish and the Ferris wheel, we went back to his apartment and made out on his couch, listening to Van Morrison until dawn. My arm fell asleep about an hour in, but I didn't say anything for fear of disrupting the kissing. When I finally got up to leave, it hurt to get my keys out of my purse.

From that day forward, the hot guy who was completely out of my league became my boyfriend. I was ecstatic, because I felt like by landing him I had achieved something. I put Jay on a pedestal before we'd ever even spoken. He had a career. He was cultured. He had a bookshelf full of hardcovers and watched foreign films that he actually liked and listened to NPR and drank wine (from a bottle, not a box). And he cooked! Like, really cooked. I think he poached a salmon at one point.

I was equally fascinated and intimidated by him. At this point I was working retail at Pottery Barn with no plan for the future, and I hadn't been exposed to movies with subtitles or unboxed wine. I didn't know how to boil water, let alone poach a fish. Needless to say, I was not in the power position in this relationship.

When I feel insecure in a romantic relationship, I tend to unravel quite quickly. At least that was true at the time. My signature move was to pack up all my opinions, feelings, likes, and dislikes, and set them aside so I could absorb the lifestyle, interests, and friends of whoever I was dating. *If I remain compliant, sweet, easy, and suggestible, then you'll really love me, right?*

To be clear, no boyfriend ever so much as implied they wanted me to do them this kindness, and in the end, in fact, they were all repelled by it. If I had no self-worth, how could anyone else value me? Somehow, though, I was able to squeeze an eight-month relationship out of Jay. In the mornings we drank coffee and read the newspaper, on weekends we had dinner parties with his friends, and a few nights a week, we'd have sex—sometimes with the lights on. It all felt very adult, and for a little while there I thought this thing had legs.

Of course, I was kidding myself, and pretty much as soon as I exposed him to my many emotional issues— insecurity, a lack of direction, depression, neediness—it was over. But before he broke up with me, Jay suggested I go to therapy. It was probably a gentle suggestion, but I imagine somewhere in his mind he was like, "You're a clingy, needy, codependent mess, and I am not up for the challenge of dealing with it, so let me at least get you into therapy." It was great advice, coming from a good man, and while it broke my heart wide open, it actually put me on a path to personal and professional success. I know now that when your boyfriend—or anyone else who loves you—suggests that you go into therapy, it's not necessarily just a kind gesture, it's because they think you need help. But since I was young and naive, I looked at Jay's suggestion as more of an investment on his part, like he saw real potential and that I just needed to be fiddled with in order to make "us" work.

Up until that point, I had a strong aversion to therapy. When I was a teenager, my mother dragged me, my dad, and my little brother to see her psychologist in an effort to torture us or align us as a family, depending on who you ask. We were bribed to go with the promise of Fuddruckers cheeseburgers and fries, which got us in the car, but because the three of us really didn't want to be there, we basically refused to participate in the session.

"Was it as awful as I remember?" I asked my mom recently, when discussing this memory.

"It was awful because you didn't want to go," she said. "While we were in there you didn't participate, and your brother didn't participate."

"Did Dad participate?"

"No," she said.

"So it was a hostage situation?"

"I remember dragging you in by your hair," my dad said.

"It was the kind of thing where you were holding on to the doorjamb with all your might," my mom added.

"I think I remember. Did I put my feet up on the doorjamb like a starfish to make it impossible to push me through?" I asked.

"No, but Jason did that once as a little kid when we were trying to extract him from the video-rental place," my dad said. "Do you remember that, Saerina?"

"Yeah, I do," my mom said. "It was in the porno section."

The intention of the therapy trip, my mother later told me, was to give her therapist the chance to witness our family dynamic, so he could improve how we related to one another. We just sat there, silent, which meant everyone left angry and the therapist still didn't understand us. Or maybe he did. Maybe seeing our reaction was all the information he needed.

Like everything a parent forces on a teenager, therapy lodged itself in my brain as something I Did Not Do. But Jay wrote the names of two psychologists on a piece of notebook paper and handed it to me with a sort of "good-bye and good luck" expression on his gorgeous face. Still oblivious to his true intentions, I didn't notice that look, and, eager to please him, I had an appointment with the first therapist on the list just a few days later. Efficiency always showed up when it came to boyfriends—I can only imagine where I'd be had he said, "Girl, you better get a job."

During our one meeting, that first therapist did a lot of talking and not a lot of listening. When I wasn't sure how to articulate my feelings, she told me how I felt, which made me uncomfortable because her reasons were not resonating at all. I didn't know it yet, but I was looking for someone to empower me by extracting my strength and my story, not spin a narrative that didn't fit. She wasn't right for me at all, and had it not been for my desire to please Jay, I would have been too discouraged to call the second one.

But the second therapist . . . well, the second therapist was Laurel. Just quickly, here's a list of the people I have wanted to be in my life: Olivia Newton-John, Christie Brinkley, Chevy Chase, Belinda Carlisle, a girl from my high school who looked like Belinda Carlisle, and Laurel. She was tall and beautiful, always very well dressed and carried herself with an assuredness that I hoped was contagious. Her office felt safe and bright, and when we first met, she offered me tea and tissues. Moments later, I sat on her green velvet couch, took a sip of Earl Grey, and told her everything.

When Laurel asked me questions she looked into my eyes with such attentiveness and genuine curiosity that for the first time in my life, I felt seen. For a girl who had felt incredibly misunderstood by the one most important female figure in her life, this was the gift I needed to set me on my path.

In the first few sessions, Laurel and I traipsed through

my family history and—after Jay officially broke up with me, because of course—we put a Band-Aid on my broken heart so we could start to tackle bigger issues first. Week after week, I drove an hour from my apartment in Studio City to her office in Westwood, and I sat in the waiting room, or what I liked to call "the emotional holding tank," before our appointment began. Oftentimes a group of therapists share office space, which means there might be someone else in the waiting room, watching you struggle to find the restroom key or sitting in silence while you both pretend to read magazines. *Should I recognize that you're here, or should this remain anonymous? Should I listen to the awkward conversation you're having with your husband in regard to your marriage counseling, or pretend I can't hear?* These are the questions you might find yourself considering. Thankfully this discomfort is short-lived, because therapists are quite precise about timing.

I liked and respected Laurel more than I had any other authority figure in my life, so I craved her approval and worked really hard to get it. The passion she had for her work was an emotion I hadn't witnessed that closely before, and it was inspiring. She was incredibly curious about medication, mental illness, nutrition, and alternative medicine, and she brought her learnings to me every single week. Laurel became more than just a therapist to me—she was a mentor, a life coach, and a nutritionist. She was basically a second mom, but without the personality conflict, communication problems, or overall creative differences. At one point, half joking and half absolutely not joking, I asked her if I could call her mom.

"Nope," she said, but with an appreciative smile.

Okay, I'm going to get a little prescriptive here, because I can't help myself and also because finding a therapist who's a good fit for you is more important than almost everything in life except maybe finding a great-fitting pair of jeans, which I haven't figured out the solution to yet, so I'll stick with therapists. It's really quite similar to dating, in that you have to approach it with an open mind, acknowledge there will be awkward moments, and recognize that the more you put in, the more you get out. As with dating, you're looking for a strong connection and great chemistry. Don't just pick the first one you meet, even if that's who you end up with. Meet at least two. Remember, this is someone to whom you'll be telling your innermost thoughts—secrets that go way beyond "I squeeze the toothpaste from the middle of the tube, and sometimes I think my cat is going to kill me."

You want someone whose words resonate with you deeply. Who you trust and feel comfortable with, because, week after week, you'll be spilling your guts out onto a table like puzzle pieces to be sorted through and reassembled. If you're lucky, it will end up being one of those cute puzzles with a picture of kittens in a basket. My puzzle felt more like one from a thrift store, where halfway through you realize it's missing several pieces and the lid is actually from a different puzzle and that's why it's been so complicated.

How do you know if you should see a therapist? In my opinion, if you're asking the question, you already know the answer. But you have to want it to work, and you have to be ready to do some work, because it takes time and dedication, and it will on occasion be very painful and uncomfortable. If it's not, you might need a new therapist.

Laurel was exceedingly patient, empathetic, and insightful. Though her constructive criticism was initially tough for me to take, I eventually came to welcome her no-bullshit approach. She coupled brutal honesty with nurturing compassion, and it resonated.

My main job in therapy was to be honest, take responsibility for the role I played in my problems, and work with Laurel to identify and implement solutions. Taking this sort of ownership was often difficult for my sensitive spirit, but admitting to being an active participant in your problems means you can also be an active participant in your solutions. Working with Laurel, I felt empowered and I became passionate about pursuing self-improvement. Laurel's way of attacking my problems worked for me; it was gradual and systematic, which made it feel manageable.

Because I was still hopping from one job to the next without any sort of consistent paycheck, my parents agreed to pay for my therapy. But that generosity came with strings. Namely, they felt they had the right to get involved—both to question the process and to ask my therapist for advice. I recently found a letter that Laurel wrote to my parents (with my permission), clearly in response to a note they sent her expressing concern about the fact that they were still financially supporting me.

Here's the letter, offered with some helpful translations, in case you don't speak therapist.

Dear Dr. and Mrs. Tauritz,

I received your letter and have discussed your concerns, in general, with Jennifer. I did not share the letter itself.

Again she has given permission for me to communicate with you openly.

I have similar concerns about Jennifer's ability to plan well and take care of herself financially. She exhibits less focus, accomplishment and self-reliance than I would expect for someone of her intelligence and abilities. I believe that this "stance" of Jennifer's has roots in the family system as a whole, and specifically, in her self-concept as an outgrowth of this system. [Translation: With all due respect, Jennifer is a spoiled baby, and it's your fault.] *Jennifer is just now becoming aware of these dynamics and has made a huge conceptual leap in just six sessions. The next step is change.* [Translation: I can take it from here, guys. Your daughter, although codependent and spoiled rotten, is a FUCKING GENIUS. Wait till I get done with her.]

In terms of your current and future participation in her financial support, let me be blunt. If you pull the complete financial support from her now I believe that you will engender many feelings that will be hard to overcome in the future. [Translation: She will flip her fucking lid and probably set your house on fire.] *I think it might feel like betrayal after the level of support to which she has been accustomed. Given that she's not*

stealing your electronics for drugs, we probably don't
need to take a "tough love" approach. Rather, I would
hope that the two of you could agree upon a level of
partial support for some period of time that you are
willing to give, with the aim for you to gradually wean
down and reduce this. These expectations should be
communicated to Jennifer.

In the past, Jennifer has not had the benefit of
psychotherapy and has only managed her symptoms
with psychotropic medication. I am trying to "manage"
nothing but, instead, believe that we are at the head of
her depression and low self-esteem. I will do my best
to help her believe in herself, get focused, take risks
and become more independent, both emotionally and
financially. It took 25 years for her to develop such a
fixed and self-sabotaging style. It will take some time
to turn it around.

Jennifer will probably need to divulge less of her
thinking and report less on her activities and efforts.
More independence and self-reliance means some
distance from you for now. [Translation: Um, go
ahead and lose her number.] I would like to help her
substitute a healthy intimacy for the existing intimacy
based on dependence and inadequacy. While I cannot

predict the future with any certainty, I do hope that
you will see some substantial changes with the next
6 months.
    Sincerely,
    Laurel

What Laurel outlined in the letter was going to be no small feat, and it would take a hell of a lot longer than six months, but we were both highly engaged and up for the challenge. For the first three-ish months, we dug into how my upbringing, brain chemistry, genetics, and life experiences shaped who I was and informed my current status as a lost, sensitive, codependent, immature twenty-something burdened by feelings of inadequacy and with a burning need to feel and look perfect that was having the complete opposite effect.

We spent a lot of time trying to resolve these issues and chart a course for my "professional wellness" (by that I mean figuring out what I wanted to do for a living, actually doing it, and starting to support myself). As you know, this kept us busy. And it was hard. I felt a range of emotions over the course of my time with Laurel, including shame, resentment, anger, and forgiveness. I learned to own my issues, emotions, and reactions, which involved accepting responsibility for my shortcomings and for my contributions (good and bad) to all my relationships—family, friends, boyfriends.

As time passed and we made progress, Laurel and I decided to tackle something even bigger: my depression diagnosis. Within our first six months together, she helped me find a psychiatrist. I had been on Prozac for years, unmonitored by a doctor, and it seemed that it was no longer helping. Laurel knew that there were many other antidepressant options available to me, and by that point she also suspected that I had undiagnosed ADD and anxiety. (Man, she was good.)

Finding a good psychiatrist is just as important as finding a good therapist because, like your therapist, you will be speaking to them about personal stuff. But you won't have the luxury of an hour a week. Also, you should know that psychiatrists are kind of weird. In my experience, they have more character and quirk than most doctors have in their pinky toe, which can make it harder or easier to connect with them, depending on your personality.

When you first see a psychiatrist, you usually have one long initial intake appointment followed by monthly and then quarterly appointments. The intake is around two hours, during which the doctor will inquire about your family and personal history, ask a bunch of questions about your symptoms, and maybe even have you take a test or two to help diagnose your specific issue. It helps if you go in knowing as much of this information as possible, including your physical and emotional symptoms, any specific experiences that help illustrate your issues, family history, medications you are taking or have taken and whether they worked. Personal insights are also helpful, since like all doctors, psychiatrists aren't mind readers, and in this case, that's a real shame. Hopefully somewhere out there there's a tiny wizard, in a tall pointy hat, living in a castle on a remote mountaintop creating a glitter-filled crystal ball that reads minds, but from what I can tell, nothing yet. With Laurel's help and guidance I had a lot of that information ready, which meant getting my diagnosis right would be very easy.

I'm kidding, it sucked.

So here's where it gets murky for me, partly because it was more than twenty years ago and partly because my brain got so fucked from the stress of trying to grow up and the effects of all the different drugs that I was prescribed over the next several years. Thankfully you aren't going to fact-check me, but I feel compelled to come clean. Still, what follows is my best memory of how it all unfolded.

My first mission was to find a psychiatrist who was available to see me and didn't cost four hundred dollars an hour. After some failed attempts, Laurel and I found someone, but as with most situations in life, I got what I paid for. I would go through several more psychiatrists that were also affordable (not cheap, but maybe two hundred dollars an hour instead of four hundred) before landing in the right spot.

One of the first doctors I saw was able to confirm, after an interview and a long written questionnaire, that I was suffering from ADD, as Laurel and I suspected. The ADD was definitely hampering my ability to lock into a job and also made it really hard to succeed at the jobs I did get.

Enter Adderall. This is a book, so unfortunately, I can't include the *duh duh duh duhhhhh* music that occurs when a villain arrives in the narrative. Adderall is basically like Sam Rockwell's character in the 2000 movie version of *Charlie's Angels*. First, you should know, Sam Rockwell is on my "list." And yes, of course Ryan Gosling is on there too, duh, but Sam Rockwell has stayed at the top for a long time, just above Chevy Chase in *Fletch*. But anyway, in *Charlie's Angels*, Sam's character seems sweet and innocent and helpful, enough so that Drew Barrymore's character sleeps with him, even though that is obviously against corporate policy. Then, just when she gets comfortable, he tries to kill her. And you want to hate him, because he's a manipulative, maniacal devil person, but he's still strangely kind of hot. In short, Adderall was like having sex with Sam Rockwell—good luck finding that sentence in any other mental health memoirs.

As you probably know, Adderall is a stimulant that can enhance your ability to pay attention or stay focused on an activity. At the beginning, it was fucking fantastic. I found a mental focus that had eluded me my entire life. One of the first days I took it, I spent the entire day cleaning and organizing my apartment. I even organized my spices. This from someone who could make sorting through one junk drawer a three-week project. At the end of that day I called my mom to tell her I was saved, that my life moving forward would be perfect and that I couldn't believe that people just felt like this naturally. I later found out that most people don't feel like that naturally, because it's not natural and they aren't on an amphetamine rocket fuel that sends them into concentration hyperdrive. Most people just go about their day, with normal levels of focus, and never consider moving the cinnamon next to the coriander.

The Adderall was encouraging my brain to release higher levels of dopamine so that my mood was elevated and I felt incredibly creative. In those early days on the drug, I concepted and completed several personal projects, took on a second assisting job, combed the want ads for creative job opportunities, and called a lot of people that I hadn't spoken to in years to emphatically express to them how much I loved them because ADDERALL IS SPEED. In my opinion, it's as dangerous as a street drug, and it hurt me more than it helped. The worst part wasn't the seemingly never-ending dry mouth or the chronic insomnia or even the severe loss of appetite (I couldn't consume anything other than those Ensure protein shakes, but at least I had something to chat about with my grandma, who also drank them). It was the intensifying of the anxiety that had laid relatively dormant for years. The anxiety attack I had in the airport in college was the most extreme that I had experienced thus far, which is not to say I had no anxiety at all, I just didn't know how to identify it in its more subtle forms. But after several months on Adderall, anxiety was back with a vengeance.

One day in the midst of all this, I was out running errands for Dodd and my system was so sensitive from Adderall and whatever antidepressant I was trying at the moment (there were many after Prozac) that something as seemingly insignificant as the wind on my face spurred on a major anxiety attack. Of course it didn't fully materialize until I was stuck between two people in the checkout line at Whole Foods, quickly escalating from an uncomfortable tightening in my chest and an acute awareness of my breath to OH MY GOD I'M GOING TO DIE IN WHOLE FOODS. Which, I guess if you're going to die in a grocery store, that's the best one. Before I got better at handling my anxiety, it really was a learned response in my body. At the onset of the physical symptoms, my mind took over and quickly convinced my body that any innocent situation was life-threatening—though, as far as I can tell, the only harmful thing in Whole Foods is the price of blueberries and the free cheese.

At Laurel's urging, I let my psychiatrist know that the Adderall was causing me some real problems and that I would need something else to manage my ADD and oh, by the way, I think I may also have anxiety.

My psychiatrist agreed with me and diagnosed me with generalized anxiety disorder, which is characterized by persistent and excessive worry that often arrives unprovoked. It's different from feeling situationally anxious because, say, you overslept and are going to miss a big meeting, and it's different from feeling nervous or scared because of something that should legitimately make you nervous or scared, like speaking in front of a large crowd or coming face-to-face with a king cobra. That's not to say that these types of situations can't trigger anxiety if you have the disorder, but it's simply that, more often than not, people with generalized anxiety feel like life is just one long face-to-face meeting with that big-ass snake, while on a stage in front of five hundred strangers . . . naked.

By this point I was on psychiatrist number three or four or eight, and in addition to now being treated for generalized anxiety I was also getting bounced around from one antidepressant to another without much luck.

I was prescribed so many different pills during these years. Pills that made me fall over for no reason, pills that made me gain a bunch of weight, pills that made me lose a bunch of weight. Pills that made me talk super fast. Pills that made me feel so mad that I could punch a hole through a wall, so I did. (It was after a pizza place told me I was out of their delivery area and I WAS NOT OUT OF THE DELIVERY AREA AND I WANTED PIZZA NOW AND DON'T FUCK WITH ME WHEN I'M HUNGRY.) Luckily, I haven't felt that out of control in many years, and ordering takeout has become much easier. There were pills that made me laugh really hard and pills that made me cry really hard. Some impaired my judgment, others impaired my vision, and one combo caused me to stay up for two days straight, and I'll tell you, you start ordering some really weird shit on eBay when you're awake that long. There was even one combo that made me think my cat was speaking to my dead grandmother who was stuck in the wall that separated my bedroom from the kitchen.

Rather than taking me off the Adderall and switching me to an antidepressant like Wellbutrin, which is known to help people with ADD, my psychiatrist added in an antianxiety pill and sleeping pills. Uppers to keep me up, downers to bring me back down. It was a roller coaster, but not the Disneyland kind where you're excited but feel safe. It was more like that local carnival you come across on your way home from work, and the roller coaster is made from secondhand parts and the guy running it just got out of jail.

So now in addition to all the emotional pressures of adulthood, I was struggling with some very compromised brain chemistry. My brain was being taken to the brink, stretched and twisted in ways it had never been before.

Laurel once told me that emotional stress can be as harmful to your health as any physical ailment, because your body can't entirely discern the difference between the two, and I think, for me, the stress of figuring out what I wanted to do for a living, holding down a job, gaining financial independence, finding friends, finding a boyfriend, and working on my self-esteem, all manifested in some chronic health issues. I had the flu five times in one year and had the stamina of a really tired eighty-year-old. My constant stomach pain had me convinced I had an ulcer, but many giant glasses of barium and several X-rays proved me wrong.

Writing this now makes me realize how strong I was to make it through all that, even though at the time I felt incredibly weak and fragile. I think a lot of people might have thrown in the towel on this mental health investigation, but not me. I loved problem-solving, and I was determined to find my way out of this mess.

Throughout all this, I was still seeing Laurel, and I was always very aware that while the medications were really fucking with me, our weekly sessions were helping. We were making progress: I had an improving sense of self, and I had begun to successfully pursue my career in styling. Despite the difficulties with the meds, I still managed to catch small glimpses of a stable future.

Up until this point, I had been scrimping on psychiatrists

because they are incredibly expensive and originally Laurel and I thought that medicating my depression wouldn't be all that complicated. Obviously we were wrong. So we came up with a new strategy, which meant not only finding an exceptional psychiatrist but also doing some more work on our own to understand my thoughts and reactions. Laurel suggested I read the book *An Unquiet Mind: A Memoir of Moods and Madness* by Kay Redfield Jamison, which details her experience with bipolar disorder. I recognized so much of myself in her words and especially in some of her descriptions of mania, which I was much less versed in than depression. Jamison wrote about the very behaviors I exhibited, like unwarranted shopping sprees, anger that seemingly came out of nowhere, and the rush of ideas that I had come to associate with creativity. "When you're high it's tremendous," she wrote. "The ideas and feelings are fast and frequent like shooting stars, and you follow them until you find better and brighter ones." That recognition felt scary but also encouraging. Soon Laurel and I both started to feel pretty certain that I had bipolar disorder and not just depression, so we took our hunch to the best psychiatrist in town.

At the beginning of my appointment with the new psychiatrist, I marched into his office with a giant Ziploc bag full of all the prescription pill bottles that had failed me and dramatically poured them out onto the table as if I were presenting him with evidence of a heinous crime. (I told you I loved *Law & Order*.) This got his attention. We talked about the potential of me having bipolar disorder. He asked a ton of questions about symptoms and experiences and asked me to spend the next month charting my mood. By the end of that first session, I felt confident that this doctor was going to get the diagnosis right. His attention to detail made me feel like I was in good hands, and that turned out to be true. He ultimately diagnosed me with bipolar II, and put me on a combination of the antidepressant Wellbutrin and Lamictal, a mood stabilizer, which is the key to treating bipolar.

Let me quickly hit you with some information about bipolar disorder, especially since the term is often used incorrectly to define people's personality. Bipolar disorder is a mental illness that causes often dramatic shifts in moods. High highs (mania) and low lows (depression). It's not like being in a good mood or bad mood. With the lows, it's like "I can't taste anything, it's hard to talk, and I feel like I can't move, and I'm not even sure I want to. Actually I can't feel anything at all." On the flip side, the highs are more like, "I have more energy than I know what to do with, so I'm going to use it to have sex with strangers and then call my old roommate that I haven't talked to in years to tell her I miss her, who cares that it's three a.m." Mostly it's not fun, though at times it's very fun. Bipolar disorder comes in a few different forms, but the two most common are bipolar I and bipolar II. The first is characterized by a lot of mania, and the latter, which is what I have, is characterized by depression with hypomanic episodes. Hypomania is mood elevation, but shorter and less intense bouts than with mania.

After my new psychiatrist prescribed my new combination of medication, I felt better within about two weeks. After all that work—and years and years of suffering—the "solution" came swiftly and worked quickly.

My life was changed forever. I had a diagnosis that fit, and the right medication to keep my moods stable. It felt like a fitting reward for all my hard work and persistence, but I suspected the work would never entirely be finished and I'd need to be vigilant about maintaining this newfound healthy mindset. Still, over the course of this pursuit, I'd developed confidence, maturity, and some emotional intelligence. Most of all, I had a growing inkling that I was, in fact, resilient.

Chapter 6

A Calming Shade of Blue

One of the most complicated aspects of dealing with mental illness is distinguishing between the feelings or actions that are simply a result of your personality and those that are manufactured by your brain chemistry. There is always an interplay between the two—they feed off each other, really—and, over the years, I'm happy to say I've gotten much better at discerning between them. For people with mental health issues, the ability to pop out of your mind and get a clear perspective on what's actually going on, even if just for a moment, is a survival skill of sorts. Sometimes literally.

Broaching the topic of suicide is a big decision for me. Frankly the subject makes me uncomfortable. It's a complicated topic that needs to be treated with respect, and I understand it can be very triggering. In fact, I considered leaving the parts of my life that involved suicide out of this book entirely. Partially because I have dealt with and recovered from them, but more so because I was afraid that no matter how delicately I treated the subject matter, it could upset some readers. But that felt like withholding something from you. Plus, sadly, most of us have been affected by suicide in some way, so my hope is that by addressing my experiences—and more important, my recovery—I might inspire something in you, whether it's a new perspective, a revelation, or even an answer. I'm going to be open and honest, and I hope that my story gives you some insight, or makes you feel less alone, or prompts you to get help if you need it.

Although I'm not always great at asking for help with day-to-day issues, in my darkest moments, the rock bottom under rock bottom, I'm lucky that I've always been able to identify when things got to a place where I needed to seek out real guidance and support. But there have also been instances that were less of a cry for help and more of a cry for attention or, at the very least, acknowledgment.

Perhaps the most blatant example of the latter took place when I was twelve.

While writing a book, and also in most forms of therapy, you call upon your memory and your subconscious mind for clues. When I started to think about this chapter, the first story that popped into my head is the same one I used to tell my therapist or psychiatrists or guys on a second date (too soon, I know that now). It's funny the things you commit to your consciousness, assigning them to one category without ever revisiting or reassessing your understanding. For many years, I categorized the story I'm about to tell you as "the time I tried to kill myself when I was a kid." Which sounds like I was trivializing suicide, but in fact I was just miscategorizing a memory. Don't worry, I'm going to tell you all about it. I mean, I told a bunch of guys I never even got to second base with about it, so I'm definitely going to tell you.

Middle school is hard. Somehow I went from a cute, sweet, smart, shy fifth grader who lots of kids really liked to a cute, sweet, smart, shy sixth grader who lots of kids thought was kind of a nerd. That shyness, which had once made me approachable, now seemed more like an invitation to bulldoze me. It was a sign of weakness, and twelve-year-olds can smell weakness a mile away. And it wasn't like the bullying of today. It was more subtle and intimate. There was no internet or social media to publicly blast people. This was more like someone whispering "You're so ugly, you stupid bitch" into my ear as they passed me in the stairwell—that was a fun thing to carry with me for the next several years (or, you know, my entire life). Or it was one of the popular girls literally acting like I was invisible. Maybe that still happens in school today, in addition to the social media blasting? I don't know, but I certainly don't miss being a preteen.

Listen, don't feel too sorry for me. I had emotional struggles, but I also had fun and sunshine on my face most days so it wasn't overtly awful. And I did have friends, probably even more than I realize. One time I paired up with two of those friends—or one close friend, Elise, and one friend of hers, Tracy, who I didn't really trust—to do some standard prank calling. You know: "Is your refrigerator running? Yes? You better go catch it!" That type of stuff. At least, that's how it started. Soon we got bored by how benign those calls were and upgraded to creepy heavy breathing or saying downright inappropriate things to whoever answered the phone. During one of those calls, the person on the other end of the line recognized Tracy's voice and called her mom to rat us out. Why would we have pranked someone Tracy actually knew? I imagine it was because we were twelve and at that age you still think you can do stupid shit and not get caught. Anyway, when Tracy got home, she was in big trouble. And I suspect she was in trouble a lot, so she told her mom that the calls were all my idea and that I forced her and Elise into it. As if I held a gun to their heads, which was preposterous, because at that point in my life I couldn't convince most people that I even existed, much less get them to do something they could get in big trouble for. But her mom bought it, probably because she didn't want to deal with her own kid, so instead she went straight to my mother to give her the news about my deviant behavior.

To my dismay, my mom actually believed that the whole scheme was my idea, which really frustrated me, but was also kind of flattering—was I a badass after all? Badass or not, I was still scared because I didn't want to get grounded. But I was also embarrassed and ashamed, because I knew my parents were probably disappointed in me. And yet, instead of screaming at me, as I expected, my parents just went into the other room. I know now that they were probably discussing my punishment in private, but at the time I felt like they were going to watch TV, like they didn't even care about me enough to be angry that I'd supposedly instigated this whole elaborate prank-call scandal. You would think I'd be grateful that maybe I'd avoided punishment, but I was looking for drama. I wanted the focus back on me, because at that age I felt simultaneously like my parents paid too much attention to me and also like they completely ignored me. Adolescence is complicated.

My response to this seemingly minor incident was a strange one: I decided that I should overdose on pills. Just end it. I walked into the bathroom, opened the medicine cabinet, spent probably five minutes trying to break into the childproof lid on a bottle of Sudafed, and then attempted to overdose on four pills.

Obviously, I was not going to die from taking four Sudafed tablets, and on some level I would have known that. But I know now that this act was not actually fueled by suicidal desires. I did not truly lose the will to live, even though I've flagged this as a suicide memory for most of my life. The logical next question, of course, is why the fuck were these pills the next step for me? I've been thinking about that a lot, and here's what I've figured out: It was a cry for attention and an attempt to get out of being grounded. But still, a pretty weird path to choose. I remember feeling nervous and scared and also excited that I was going to get a big reaction from my parents. I laid down on the cream-colored Berber carpet (cream-colored carpet with two kids—were they crazy?) and placed the open bottle next to me with a few more pills spilled out onto the floor, just like I had seen on TV. Then I waited. Less of a waiting to die and more like a waiting for my parents to find me and think I was going to die and pay so much attention to me that I might explode with happiness.

But you know what? Those fuckers never came into the room. I was easily in there for almost an hour, which is a lifetime when you are a kid (and like three seconds if you're a dog) and nothing. NOTHING. Eventually I got bored of waiting and put the spilled pills back in the bottle, put the bottle away, and went back into the living room. I never even told my parents about it—in fact, they're probably learning about it for the first time as they read this book. Hi, Mom. Hi, Dad.

I know with certainty that this was not a true suicidal moment because many years later, while I was struggling to get my mental health issues figured out, I actually did lose the will to live. I was not calling out for attention, but I did eventually cry for help. Because this time it really was my brain chemistry, and even though I was lucky enough to see that, it was fucking scary.

It was during the years that I was bouncing from one job to the next, working with Laurel to get the right diagnosis and the right meds. I'd already seen some psychiatrists— including the one who diagnosed me with ADD—but I hadn't yet seen the one who would give me my bipolar diagnosis and get me the meds I needed. So at the time, I was depressed, but I also had a false sense of happiness and energy that was a direct result of the ADD medications. I was more productive than I'd ever been, but the energy was chemically induced and had an expiration, so in between jobs I would lay silent and listless on my bed for days, just trying to recoup everything I had exerted in order to seem okay.

During some of this time I felt incredibly disassociated from my body. It was similar to how I felt when I thought my skin had turned green years earlier. It's as if you aren't outside of yourself and you aren't inside of yourself—you are a blur, a semiopaque ghost of yourself stuck in limbo, feeling really high and really low and then feeling nothing at all.

A Calming Shade of Blue

It only compounded things that, at the time, I was living alone. I hadn't had a roommate for years, and I didn't have a boyfriend or any close friends who I trusted to understand my predicament (this is a common issue for people with mental health issues). Sometimes it's hard to explain to someone who doesn't suffer from depression why ice cream and a movie won't cheer you up. I remember feeling like my therapist and my mom were the only people I could talk to, and although that was two more than none, it was a lot less support than I thought I needed.

Suffering from mental illness without the support system you need feels like being on a trapeze without a net. Wait, that's too simple. It's like being on a trapeze without a net, and you're trapezing for the very first time, and the trapeze is over a giant lake, which sounds really picturesque, but the lake is full of alligators. Hungry alligators that survive solely on the salt in your tears and your tiny arms, legs, hands, and feet. Basically, they are going to eat you. So what I'm saying is, don't give up on the trapeze, just get a net, which, in this elaborate metaphor, means that you should find support. Hopefully that includes people, but maybe for now it's even simpler than that. Obviously ice cream or a movie won't get to the root of your problem, but it could give you some momentary relief. Maybe you'll see something in the movie that gives you insight into your own life. Or maybe you'll have a great conversation over ice cream that leads to a deeper friendship. Stay open to support even if it doesn't come in the way you expected it to.

Anyway, trapezing without a net is exactly how I felt at twenty-nine years old when, after being through the ups and downs of the wrong medications, compromised brain chemistry, and stress, I found myself entering one of the deepest, darkest emotional valleys of my life. This one gave the Grand Canyon a run for its money.

I hadn't felt right, mentally or emotionally, for the past few days. On a scale of one to ten, I was at a two and dropping, which I was well aware was problem territory. (By then I had established with my mother the Emotional Rating System, which I used to assess my mental and emotional well-being. This has become a critical tool for me. Check out the appendix of this book to understand how you might make it work for you.) The newest potpourri of pills that my psychiatrist had prescribed me was taking my mental state from bad to worse, not better to best. For three hours, I lay balled up on the floor in a fit of uncontrollable hysterics, which included a combination of projectile crying and high anxiety that caused my hands to cramp into fists. I essentially looked like a tear-soaked maniac who was trying to imitate a dying cat. It was scary and strange and it was one of the few times in my life where, as someone who has always enjoyed being alone, being alone felt terrifying.

I called the psychiatrist in a total panic to see what I should do. I dialed his after-hours number, and as soon as he called me back, I launched into an emotional rant about how I was feeling, but he stopped me about two minutes in.

"I'm sorry," he said. "But can you remind me who you are? I can't entirely remember you."

I was in complete shock. I didn't know how to react to his inconvenient amnesia. As I've mentioned, the trust involved in psychiatry is very similar to the trust in therapy. But it's a much more awkward relationship, because you really do have to share your feelings and fears and detail your troublesome behavior, but you're revealing all this to someone you don't see every week and who doesn't really know you at all—or, apparently, even remember you exist. Still, I'd bared my soul to this person, so the idea that my name didn't even ring a bell? I couldn't handle it. I hung up on him and collapsed onto the living room floor into a puddle of my own self-pity.

Over the next few days, I spent a lot of time lying

around on my half-made bed. I had recently painted my bedroom, ditching a pale ballet-slipper pink for a much brighter Tiffany blue, because I read somewhere that blue was supposed to be soothing. At that point, I would try anything to feel soothed. If someone had told me that shaving my head and sticking five big marshmallows up my butt every morning would be soothing, I would have done that too.

Although I was aggressively struggling with my very compromised mental health and the side effects of all my meds, I still maintained a little bit of hope. It's one of my strengths—as bad as it gets, I almost always know there's a way out. Even if I can't see it, I know it's there. I can feel it. When things get especially bad, that hope becomes just the tiniest flicker of light in the distance, but it's enough.

Sometime within a week of the botched phone call to the psychiatrist, I woke up and felt different. And not in a good way. It was unlike anything I had ever experienced. It wasn't sadness or even despair, it was a lack of feeling and an absence of will. As if everything had lost meaning and mattered so little that it wasn't even worth feeling despair. My life didn't feel worth fighting for. I had been in the depths of depression before, where you sink below sadness into a murky abyss, but this was different from even that. I felt detached not just from my emotions, but from myself. I also felt really confused, because up until that point, fighting for my own happiness was second nature, but now I was ready to accept that the flicker of light in the distance was extinguished for good.

I know now that this emotional low was caused at least in part by the fact that I was incorrectly medicated and was being treated for depression when I actually had bipolar II. Over time, when taking antidepressants alone, bipolar II can get exacerbated, and the meds can actually worsen the depression and cause thoughts of suicide. I lost the will to live, and there wasn't a shade of blue for the walls that could possibly help.

What's curious is that I actually felt it leave. The feeling of wanting to be alive, that is. It was a subtle shift, but I clocked it. There was no anger, no pain, no sorrow. And there was no solution. Or at least, no solution that sounded compelling. Instead, it was just silence and stillness, and I felt very clear and calm. Calmer than I had felt in a very very long time. I was at peace with it.

Thankfully some small part of me knew that this sensation, and my reaction to it, wasn't the real me. I wasn't someone who made peace with problems; I was a fighter. That fact that I was ready to accept defeat, that I didn't want to fight, was really a stronger red flag than the depression itself. I knew there must be a glitch somewhere inside.

Until that point in my life, I had limited experience with suicide, so I had constructed a narrative that made the subject feel palatable. People who made such a tragic choice, I told myself, must have a very clear reason. I believed there was always an external factor to blame. I know now that suicide is more complicated than this. There are many emotional and physiological ways that someone can go from okay to bad to horrible to suicidal. To anyone reading this who might be feeling that way right now: Please talk to someone *now*. No doubt you've heard this before, and maybe you've even tried it and it didn't really feel like it helped, but try again (and again and again). Right away. If you don't have a therapist or psychiatrist or someone close and reliable, call the Suicide Prevention Lifeline (1-800-273-TALK) or another suicide crisis hotline, and get support and advice.

Because I had this misunderstanding about suicide, I was especially confused by my own feelings. Sure, I was in a place of frustration and pain and figuring things out, but there was nothing I was desperately trying to escape. There was no unavoidable financial ruin or any kind of abuse. I wasn't suffering from a terminal illness. And I had never thought about suicide before. I was sure it had to be something with the meds.

Maybe it was a result of my growing self-awareness due to my therapy, but even in my lowest point, I was able to get outside of my condition for just long enough to ask for help. I didn't call my psychiatrist back—I mean, that ship had sailed. I didn't even call Laurel. I called the one person I knew would help instantly. I called my mom.

It's funny, for as vividly as I remember that day and those feelings—or lack of them—I can't remember what I said to my mom or how our conversation went. And as you might guess, she doesn't either. I just know that after discussing my options for immediate help, we decided it would be best for me to get on the next flight home to Florida and stay there until we could get it all sorted out.

Being home helped immediately, and after a few days surrounded by my parents, who I'm sure were terrified but did an incredible job of making me feel, if not better, at least safe, I started working remotely with Laurel and my psychiatrist (who was now, thankfully, aware of who I was) to rectify the situation. Over the next few weeks he weaned me off most of my meds to get a clear baseline, and that certainly helped. Thankfully, during that time, my will to live floated back into my body almost in the same way that a really bad flu floats out.

After those three weeks back home with my parents, and after getting off almost all the medications, I returned to LA, and Laurel and I got back to work. Shortly after this episode is when we tracked down the right psychiatrist and I got my bipolar diagnosis, and things got so much better from there. My brain has never been hijacked in that same way again. This is not to say I never got depressed again. I still find myself there from time to time, and I can feel quite quickly when it comes on, but luckily I know enough now to handle it better. I have a three-day rule: I allow myself to just be sad and live in that darkness. Once three days have passed, I know I have to watch myself closely. If I'm that down for a full week, it's time to call my doctor, and he always remembers who I am.

Chapter 7

This Is Just the Beginning

This chapter starts out like a love story. And, in fact, that's exactly what it is, though not the one I ever imagined for myself. You'll see what I mean. Just stick with me.

Dating in LA is the absolute worst. It will steal your soul. No, actually it will whisper cutting insults in your ear, unexpectedly punch you in the face, steal forty bucks out of your wallet, and then steal your soul. "Dating" is really a generous term for my personal experience, because I went on only about ten dates in ten years, though there were some memorable moments in there. There was the guy who laughed hysterically after he orgasmed and then turned to me and said, completely serious, "This is just something I do; you'll get used to it." Then there was the guy with whom I went on two sort of strange dates, and then, well, he died. Straight up died in his sleep. Another guy was named Herb. That's the whole story. What else do you need? His. Name. Was. Herb.

I didn't especially care that the dating scene was a bust. I've almost never been afraid to be alone—in fact, I enjoy it. I was an only child for the first seven years of my life, and in that time I grew accustomed to keeping myself company, though when my brother, Jason, was born I certainly enjoyed dressing him up like the younger sister I always wanted. But I was content enough on my own that I didn't mind watching my friends, every last one of them, fall in love and get married. My parents were a bit concerned, but I was fine.

But then, one day in my early thirties, the desire for companionship hit me. Hard. It was sudden. It was emphatic. And I have no idea what caused it. I just remember working on a styling job and shaking my hands up at the sky, yelling "Lord, please send me someone to love. I AM READY!"

Three days later, I met Andrew.

Andrew was from Australia, but he was in LA visiting

a mutual friend. We met at Mexico City—a local Mexican restaurant, not the actual city—and I was immediately drawn to him because he bore an uncanny resemblance to a guy I'd been in a brief but intense relationship with, though his kind and calm demeanor is what drew me in most. I felt safe and comfortable with Andrew right away, which is rare for me, so I let my guard down. Between that and my true desire to find a boyfriend, things moved fast. We spent almost every moment together, talking, laughing, eating, drinking, sexing. It was intense. The universe had heard my cry and delivered. Within a week, we decided to get married.

We didn't pull the trigger immediately. We almost did, going so far as to drive to Las Vegas, but in the end we realized we wanted our parents there, and we were at least wise enough to see that such an impulsive wedding might introduce more complications to the relationship than we wanted to deal with. So Andrew returned to Australia to fulfill a teaching commitment, we maintained a long-distance relationship for a year, and then, on February 14, 2005 (that was my idea, I'm a hopeless romantic), he moved to the States. A few months later we returned to Vegas and got married for real.

The first year was a fairy-tale fantasy—buying dishes,

celebrating holidays, hosting dinner parties, and saying "my husband" and "we" a lot. But we got married quickly, and it's maybe not surprising that the fairy tale wore off eventually. I'll tell you more about that later.

By the time our third anniversary came around, Andrew and I were already well into a marriage that wasn't working, but not nearly far enough in to give up hope (it would be many more years before all hope was gone, and a few years beyond that before we actually did something about it and got divorced). In those early years of our marriage, I was working pretty consistently as a prop stylist and got booked on a job over the weekend of our anniversary, in Vegas of all places. Andrew wasn't working full-time, so I convinced him to come with me for old time's sake and suggested that we do something fun and exciting like renew our vows at the drive-through wedding chapel. He agreed. It would be the first of a thousand things we did to try to resuscitate our relationship.

I had just come off some styling jobs in which my assistant, Jamie, and I used vintage flowers and ribbon as hair accessories and used actual daisies to create beautiful flower crowns. I feel compelled to point out that this was like two years before the flower-crown revolution, because obviously I want some credit for being ahead of that trend. I had a bunch of leftover materials at my house, and I wanted to create something fancy and fun to mark the occasion of our vow renewal, so I found some millinery wire and a glue gun and I sat on the floor of our living room burning my fingertips (not lighting my nails on fire, promise) while wrapping silk ribbon around the wire that I had fashioned into a halo. I attached a few big flowers and some velvet leaves, and that was that. The final product was a bit outrageous, but I had forgone wearing a veil at our wedding, so this seemed like a nice three-years-later redo.

When it comes to fashion, I've always had a strong sense of style. I know what I like and what I want to wear, and I don't care if it's on trend. I'm one of those people who only utters the words "I could never pull that off" in regard to a thong bikini or a pencil skirt (hellooo, hips that don't lie and ass that won't quit). But bold patterns, sequins, or statement accessories? I'm all in!

Andrew and I arrived at the Hard Rock Hotel, got upgraded to a suite, and prepared to renew our vows. I did my hair and makeup, put on my favorite dress from Anthropologie, and placed my new floral halo atop my head. We got in the car, drove up to the chapel window in our Volkswagen Jetta, and instead of handing us cheese-burgers and fries, a nice minister leaned out the window and remarried us in under two minutes flat.

Andrew wasn't embarrassed by the giant thing on my head, exactly, but he was not 100 percent comfortable with it either. As we walked into the casino after renewing our vows, he looked at me and asked, "Are you going to wear that all night?"

The answer was a resounding yes. I felt awesome in it. And I liked that it piqued people's curiosity. Through-out the night, several drunk women fell over themselves complimenting me on it, and several drunk men looked at me like I had a very rare, exotic bird on my head. A week or so later, I posted a Polaroid that Andrew had taken of me on my photography blog, and the response was more emphatic than I'd seen on any other post. The comments were filling up with people asking if they could pay me to make them one too. *Well this is different*, I remember thinking. *Maybe I should start selling them.*

A few days later, Jamie texted me a picture from her thirtieth birthday party and right there on her head was an extremely similar masterpiece to the one I had created. We hadn't discussed the fact that we were both making these headpieces, and I distinctly remember feeling kind of tingly when I saw her photo, because I knew we were onto something.

The fact that Jamie and I each wore a headpiece for such significant occasions convinced me that we had tapped into the creative consciousness. I have always viewed ideas as energy, floating in and out of our minds and in the air around us. Whether or not we choose to harness that energy is what differentiates us. Creatives tend to harness it more, both because we're trained to and because we're paid to. I look for ideas all the time and everywhere—when I drive, when I watch TV, when I go to the grocery store or a museum, or even when I scroll on Instagram. And since technology has connected society today more than ever, it's easy for big groups of people to simultaneously tap into the same collection of ideas. That's how trends happen, and the only way to get ahead of a trend—which I felt like we were on the cusp of doing with the headbands—is to follow your gut immediately, without too much deliberation or complication.

So that's what we did. I told Jamie that some of my blog readers had inquired about buying the headpieces and that I was thinking of pursuing it, and she said she was considering selling some too. We had worked together for years and always got along really well, although we rarely took that chemistry beyond work hours to see each other socially, since she was more inclined to stay in with friends and her husband watching movies or playing improv games, while I usually opted to go out with friends and without my husband, drinking until it seemed logical to do a backbend on a couple of small cocktail tables. I thought this was the perfect working relationship—I assumed it would protect us from the whole "don't mix business with pleasure" trap. And so we decided to start a company.

The very next day, and for the next two months, Jamie and I split our time between styling jobs and our new headband business. We spent nights and weekends painstakingly creating a thirty-piece collection of one-of-a-kind, elaborate headpieces and took a week to brainstorm a name. In the end we were choosing between Bandeaux, the French word for "headband," and Halo, because most of our pieces were built off a ribbon-covered wire halo. We ultimately chose Bandeaux but changed it to ban.do because I thought that seemed unique. In retrospect, this was not the best decision—ban.do is hard to type and 50 percent of people think it's pronounced bandoo. But there's no turning back now. Trust me, I've tried.

This Is Just the Beginning

The nice thing about starting ban.do when I did was that styling had given me a great education in aesthetic and photography—both of which are integral to e-commerce. Etsy was huge at the time, and we considered going that route, but my brother was a graphic designer and knew some simple front-end coding, and Jamie's husband could do some more sophisticated back-end work (that's what she said), so we decided to go out on our own. I wish our first site were still live today, just so I could flag how unsophisticated it was. There was a splash page (I don't know if anyone remembers splash pages, but they were basically intro landing pages that you saw before you clicked into the main site—they were cool for about a minute and also completely useless), and we had pretty much no SEO (search engine optimization), which meant we barely came up in a Google search. Ours was sort of the opposite of what you want an e-commerce site to be, which, in many ways, turned out to be great.

Like most start-ups, we called in lots of free help from friends and family, and when I say "called in help" I mean we used a series of veiled threats, guilt trips, and free wine, so everyone eventually said yes. Andrew kept us fed and ran errands, and was kind enough to tolerate Jamie and me turning the entire front section of our house into a makeshift production studio / creative office space / distribution center. My brother and I laid a lot of creative groundwork for the brand, including concepting a simple but unique design for the website and coming up with the first ban.do logo. (I've come to learn that when it comes to these creative business decisions, oftentimes your first instinct is right. That doesn't mean you won't explore a boatload of versions, but you almost always come back to the idea that quickly followed the point of inception.) Our friend Bobbi had beautiful handwriting and loved free wine, so we convinced her to handwrite the original haikus we came up with to accompany each piece in the collection. Yes, you read that right, all orders came with an original haiku. Clearly we had no growth strategy, and eventually we figured out that handwritten notes don't really scale, so we sadly had to let them go. All the while, Jamie and her husband, Pete, worked night and day to set up the e-commerce side of the website, open bank accounts, and apply for a business license—all the logistical and administrative work that wasn't my strong suit and still isn't my strong suit. It was my first glimpse of a business lesson I would come to learn all too well: creatives often need logistical and operational support so we can focus on being creative and not be eye-tortured by spreadsheets.

This Is Just the Beginning

We were excited about ban.do but, in those early days, it was less of a calculated business endeavor and more of a half-baked creative project, one that was born long before stories of female founders and girl bosses were constantly making headlines. There was certainly no business plan or venture capital or any real experience to speak of. What we had was a lot of positive energy focused on filling our downtime with creativity, making beautiful things with our hands, and connecting with people through our work. Oh, and eventually becoming millionaires, but we both acknowledged how far-fetched that was. We let our hearts and guts make most of the decisions and financed the business with blood, sweat equity, and tears. As far as actual money goes, we each put in three hundred dollars and, I guess I'll admit this now, we used some money left over from a Nordstrom catalog photo shoot budget (from a styling job we both worked on) and bought bags of vintage flowers and beautiful silk ribbon to make our initial pieces. Hopefully there's a statute of limitations that will protect me from any sort of prosecution—thank you, Nordstrom!

The morning we launched the site was so exciting. We just sat there, refreshing our email browsers and waiting for the first sale to come in. We had friends who ran popular blogs at the time, and they all covered our launch and drove a lot of traffic to the site—special shoutout to Joy Cho, founder of Oh Joy!, for single-handedly building our business and yes she paid me to put this note in here. After about thirty minutes, the first order came in. And then another. And then another and another, and by the end of the first day—or second day maybe, I can't remember but I know it was early—we had sold out. Since everything was one-of-a-kind, our prices were much higher than today's ban.do prices. The headpieces were going for $95 to $350 a pop, so we knew we were going to be RICCCCHHHH BITCHHHHHH and maybe become millionaires after all. That is, until we ran the numbers and realized how expensive it is to run a business (gross profit versus net profit, these are the things I learned later on). But for a day or two, we were rich. Like quit-our-jobs and buy-fancy-shoes rich. Shortly afterward we got the jobs back and returned the shoes. Fine, I didn't return the shoes.

For the first few weeks and months, things were great. We could barely keep up with the orders and worked frantically to fill them. It was thrilling. Each piece was unique, and we continued to charge accordingly, and people just kept coming. Jamie and I cut back on our styling work to dedicate more time to the business.

Although I was on meds, I was still actively dealing with my mental health issues. That's kind of how it goes with mental illness, especially when you factor in the new-business-owner lifestyle of less sleep and a diet that consists primarily of pizza. Anxiety, specifically, was playing a starring role in my personal life, and something as simple as taking my dog for a walk could result in a full-on panic attack. Phil loves walks more than I love pasta, and, lucky for him, I walk to clear my head—and also to get at least fifteen minutes of sunlight in my eyes each day. I think it's good for me, and also a doctor once told me, "It's good for you." Once, while Phillip and I were on our daily stroll, we mutually decided to go down a street we'd never been down before, and halfway down that really quiet street—like, zombie-apocalypse quiet—I saw a man slowly heading down his driveway, walking toward us, carrying a green Weedwacker. He was about six feet tall, narrow face, medium-brown hair, light eyes, a well-kept mustache and a five o'clock shadow, and wearing cobalt-blue sweatpants and a red-and-blue sports jersey. It could have been a Patriots jersey, not sure. If you're wondering why I just described him as if I were talking to a police sketch artist, it's because I thought that was a real possibility.

Knowing this guy was most likely a murderer, what with the Weedwacker and my innate ability to jump to the worst-case scenario, I hurried Phil down the sidewalk in an effort to stay alive, because I suddenly had the distinct feeling that he was about to run after us and start chopping us both in half. I quickly surveyed the empty street. *I'm gonna die on this empty street, chopped in half, lying in a pool of blood next to my chopped-in-half dog, and this guy's gonna get away with it.* When the man got to the sidewalk, he just walked in the other direction without murdering us.

All of this took maybe six seconds. But they were six very impactful seconds.

Passing men with Weedwackers makes me anxious. Really anxious. On a bad day, the wind blowing in my face makes me anxious. So does making unprotected lefts on the streets of LA and not finishing my to-do list on any given day. Also, parking garages. I have literally run screaming through parking garages, flailing my arms, just to make sure no one kills me. Meanwhile, in those moments, I'm sure I'm the one who looks like a murderer.

In some ways, the anxiety that was my Achilles' heel in my personal life became my superpower when it came to ban.do. I'd been seeking some version of shiny perfection ever since my mom told me I wasn't a diamond, and this felt like one area that I really could get perfect, as long as I held the reins. For a bit, it seemed like I was right. That anxiety—and my desire to avoid an anxiety attack— propelled me to double- and triple-check every product and every form and every label, and also to question every decision. This helped us avoid a lot of mistakes and keep the business moving at a healthy pace, but it also drove the people around me crazy. I know this because later, once the company had grown a bit, every time I entered our shipping center (less of a center and more of a closet, who am I kidding?) to triple-check that the right products were in the right boxes, and that tissue paper was folded correctly, and that the silk ribbon, at the exact right length, was tied in a neat bow around the tissue paper, the sweet kid who did our shipping tried so hard not to roll his eyes back into his head that he practically convulsed.

Also, after suffering with depression for so long, I found myself seeking out things that brought me joy. I craved bright colors and designs that conveyed optimism, and this desire guided us in a lot of our early decision-making. What seemed outlandish to some people brought Jamie and me so much happiness, and it turned out to do the same for others. It also helped that by this time, after years of working with Laurel and nurturing my own increasing interest in mental health, I had developed a good amount of emotional intelligence. This ability to recognize my own emotions and also have empathy for others enabled me to innately understand what would resonate with customers. I could sense it almost viscerally, and it seemed that my sensitivity and struggles pointed us in the right direction. And I understood what it was we were serving the customer—we were inspiring fun and eliciting joy, which was the true intention of the brand. And that was the case long before we sold the business and expanded to lifestyle products like planners and pool floats and mugs that very overtly check those boxes.

A few months later, reeling from our early success, we decided it was time to button up this operation and move from my living room floor into a proper office space. Jamie and I were really excited about the opportunity to grow the business, and Andrew was equally excited, because he had had enough of living in a headband factory. While I was working on a big styling job in San Diego, Jamie scoured Craigslist and found us a really cute space on the second floor of a small office building in Hollywood, right off Beverly and Fairfax. She was very task-oriented and was exceptional at completing a to-do list, no matter the size. If it was up to me to find an office, we'd still be in the living room.

Our new offices used to belong to Steve Martin and Rob Reiner or some other comic geniuses, and in the forties, the building was all doctors' offices. My sense is that plenty of people died in those offices because the building was most definitely haunted, something the landlord failed to mention when we signed our lease. Every now and then we would hear strange phantom sounds or just get the feeling that there was a presence, LIKE A FUCKING GHOST, among us. One night, when Jamie and I were alone in the building working late, I heard a noise that sounded like someone walking in the hall outside our office. I looked up to see who it was, and through the beveled glass on the door that looked out into a shared rotunda, I saw a slightly distorted image of a man walk by. And he wasn't wearing a shirt, which was strange, exciting, and also quite terrifying.

"Um, Jamie, is anyone still here?" I asked.

"Nope, everyone left," she said.

"Okay, that's weird, because I just saw a topless man walk by our door."

Jamie, looking like she was about to pass out, said nothing and just stared at me. We grabbed our glue guns and wire cutters—the only weapons we had on hand—and opened our door just enough to yell through the opening.

"Hello?"

Silence.

"Anybody there?"

Silence.

Much braver than I, Jamie stepped into the hall and flipped on the light. There was no one there, but there definitely hadn't been enough time for anyone to leave. So we did what any rational people would do and threatened murder into the empty void. "We know you're in here! We are armed and dangerous!" Then we grabbed our purses, a bag of Skittles (because, you know, Skittles), and ran out of the office. We never stayed that late again.

So, sure, the building was haunted, but it was also incredibly charming, and charming beats terrifying in the design world every single time. There was a lot to love about our seven hundred square feet, except the wall-to-wall carpeting, which looked like it had been the site of several violent crimes. We had managed to save some money for office improvements, so once we signed the lease, the first order of business was pulling out that carpet and painting the floor underneath it with a high gloss white to really "open up the space." We did that over a weekend, and late that Sunday night Andrew and I left to drive to San Diego, back to that same styling job. The next day, I got a call from Jamie, who warned me she had bad news. Of all the different kinds of news, I hate bad news the most. My anxiety ran me through all the worst-case scenarios. Death. Robbery. Murder. Fire. But it was worse. Well, it wasn't, but it seemed that way for a moment.

Turned out that unbeknownst to us, there were several small holes in our office floor, which happened to also be the ceiling of one of the most expensive shops in LA. Three tiny drops of our paint had seeped through the floor and dripped onto a chair and ottoman with a combined value of $15,000. The owner of the shop, who, with all due respect, ended up being a top-notch asshole, was insisting we reimburse him the full amount. We didn't have $15K. We didn't have $1K. We were fucked.

Just to be clear, I'm not saying this guy was an asshole because he wanted us to pay for the damage we caused, I'm saying he was an asshole because he was completely unsympathetic and unwilling to help us find a viable solution. And when we went down to see him in person and apologize, he had us wait outside his office for thirty minutes and then told his assistant to send us away because he decided he wasn't interested in talking to us after all.

After weeks of back-and-forth we convinced him to settle on an amount that was less than $15,000 but still a lot more than we could afford.

It was the first of many "one step forward, four steps back" scenarios that we would encounter as business owners, but we took it in stride, though sometimes when he had a high-profile customer in his shop we'd place a speaker near one of the holes in the floor and blast N.W.A.

In the first few years of ban.do we learned so much and struggled so much and faced some big financial lessons— like when you stop taking paid work and instead dedicate your time to a company that pays you in sweat equity rather than actual money, you might lose or sacrifice some things. Like your house. As you can probably guess, I mean that literally. Andrew and I lost to foreclosure the very house in which we started ban.do during those early years. Andrew was struggling to find meaningful work, and I was so caught up in ban.do—and so low on salary—that we couldn't pay the mortgage. And we didn't miss just a month or two. We didn't pay our mortgage for a full year. After negotiating with the bank for another year after that, we lost the house, and honestly it felt like a relief rather than a failure. It was certainly the kind of loss that might send someone into a tailspin, but as soon as the pressure of owing all that money, and not knowing how I would ever pay it back, was off, I felt like I could breathe again. Sure, I was breathing in a shitty rental, out $80,000 with nothing to show for it, but even that never made me want to give up on ban.do. It always always always felt like the solution and not the problem. On paper that made no sense, but deep in my gut it did. Eventually, after we'd had the business for a couple of years, Jamie and I decided to each take a $1,000-a-month salary.

It wasn't all struggles and misery, obviously. We had some wins in that time, and they always came right as we were starting to wonder how we could possibly stay in business. We did the small and seemingly obvious growth stuff, like divide and conquer rather than do everything together, and we grew our team and started hiring employees. Natalie, the first hire, came on to do design. Her interview went something like this:

Us: Hi. Can you sew?
Natalie: Yes.
Us: You're hired!

Kelly came next. She was hired to "help anywhere she can."

Us: What kind of job are you looking for?

Kelly: I'm not sure; I just want to help.

Us: Cool, can you work for eleven bucks an hour?

Kelly: Twelve?

Us: You're hired!

We brought on a bunch of interns, some of whom stayed for a few months, others for a couple of years. My favorite intern, Christina, left for a bit for a better-paying job but eventually was hired back as our director of social media. We held her job interview in a tiki bar and sealed the deal over a couple of blue hawaiians, if that's any indication of the level of professionalism we were operating at. We were a small but mighty team of perfectionists, doing the work of many, but we built a real closeness and camaraderie during that time. Natalie is still one of my closest friends and still works freelance for ban.do, and Kelly and Christina play major roles in the company even all these years later. They're part of my OG crew of ride-or-dies that I call The 7958ers (the address of our first office).

As our team grew, everything I learned over the years about professional hierarchies and how management should treat employees—don't, for example, call people "Hey you"—suddenly came flooding back to me. Turns out being an extra was good for something! And Jamie and I defined our roles more clearly: I was spearheading the creative, and she was running the business side, not because she wasn't creative, but because she could complete tasks in a timely and effective manner and because math is a four-letter word for me.

We also got an accidental brand ambassador in Taylor Swift, which, as you might imagine, was huge for us. It started when Taylor was doing a cover shoot for *Seventeen* magazine, and a stylist pulled a ban.do hairpiece for her to wear. She fell in love with it. We sent her many more at the request of her stylist, and she started wearing ban.do almost every day. I know this because there were (and probably still are) entire websites devoted to what Taylor Swift is wearing. We ended up designing pieces for her tour and creating a small capsule collection with her that was sold on her website. That endorsement really helped us get our name out there. We were also on the cover of *InStyle Weddings*, after another brand pulled their product at the last minute. That one magazine cover was enough exposure to keep our business afloat for a while. We took on an angel investor who gave us $40,000—not a huge investment but enough of a cash injection that we could keep operations up and running. And then one day we got an email from a buyer at Anthropologie, inquiring about doing business with us. It was the type of email where, as you're reading aloud, your voice keeps getting louder and louder, and by the end you're screaming and inserting *OMG!* at the end of each sentence. We set a meeting with the buyer at a fancy Santa Monica hotel, and Jamie and I put on our favorite dresses, crossed our fingers, and hoped we could woo her with our wit and charm, since we knew business acumen would not be the hook. She liked us, thank God, and we set up a call to talk details with her larger team. We were so nervous to get on the phone, but I took the lead and kept it real cool, speaking slowly, inserting a laugh in the appropriate spots, and then frantically scribbling words I should Google, like "margins," because fuck if we knew what a margin was.

Being in a store like Anthropologie involved doing actual mass production, so we got a crash course in understanding our demographic and producing overseas and shipping and distribution. We didn't make a dime from that initial deal, but it served us and our business in much larger ways.

The most important development in that time, for me personally, was that I realized ban.do had become my passion and my true love. I was head over heels, obsessed. At one point I was spending so much time at the office that Andrew actually suspected I was cheating on him. Escaping the challenges of our marriage to focus on something that gave me a huge emotional return on my investment? Sure. But no, not cheating. I was just pouring everything I had into growing and improving this company. No matter what was going wrong or how hard it was, ban.do was the only thing I wanted to do. And I do think that this almost unhealthy commitment is what it takes. Building a business is fucking hard, so if you're going to try, it really has to be your sole purpose. It doesn't have to stay that way forever—in fact letting go a little over the last few years has helped me a lot—but in the early days it needs all your attention.

In year three, Jamie decided that she was going to move to Texas because her husband had started a successful business there and he had been traveling back and forth for the better part of a year. By that point, our relationship had gotten pretty strained. Building a company from the ground up can do that to people, even if you were sure you'd avoid such a fate by starting the business with someone you didn't have a social relationship with in the first place. But even with my foolproof business-partner plan, the tensions between Jamie and me were growing.

Like I've already said, but it bears repeating, business is hard. Figuring out how to grow the business, make more money, hire a team . . . there are so many decisions to be made, and it's nearly impossible to see eye-to-eye on everything. And even if you do agree on most things, there are also different personalities and different work ethics to contend with. Different values might emerge as your business starts growing, or different coping skills might not jibe when you come up against a challenge. There are endless differences that can cause hostility. I can't speak for Jamie, but I imagine she felt like I was overbearing with my ideas and less willing to hear hers. She might say that I wrestled control of the creative side, or that I was too emotional in the workplace, or that she resented that I started taking on styling jobs when I ran out of money. (She and I discussed that last bit in advance, but I'm sure it was frustrating for her to be in the office holding down the fort while I was out working another gig.)

For my part, I was struggling both financially and mentally. I felt stressed and overwhelmed, which is pretty much a guarantee that funny, smiley, easygoing Jen will take a back seat to humorless, impatient, ragey Jen. Case in point: Toward the end of our partnership, Jamie went through what I liked to call "the apple phase," where she brought in an apple the size of a grapefruit every day and would sit at her desk eating it slowly and loudly over the course of several hours. Our office was really small, and our desks were basically touching. We all worked in the same room, so there was no privacy. I wasn't in a great place mentally, but instead of dealing with that in any kind of productive way, I hyper-focused on that apple and the incredibly irritating noise that came out of Jamie's mouth every time she took a bite, which surprisingly did not cause anyone else an ounce of discomfort. (That should have been my first clue that this was about me, not about the apple.) Each bite just made me madder and madder and madder, and there were hundreds of bites, so after hours of struggling to keep my shit together I finally turned to face her and, in a voice much deeper and more sinister than my normal one, said, "Jamie, if you take one more bite of that fucking apple, I'll strangle you to death with my bare hands and shove it down your fucking face." It wasn't my proudest moment. She just looked at me, shocked and disappointed, and slowly, without a word, put the apple down on her desk, never losing eye contact. In that moment, I knew whatever was left of our personal relationship was ruined, and part of me is still sad about that. While we were never close personal friends, we *were* business partners who built something great together. Yet I do believe we made the right choice. I can't say for certain, but I think and hope she does too.

Since I wouldn't be able to run the business on my own when Jamie moved to Texas, we decided to look into selling. It was an easy decision—we wanted to stay in business, and we knew that the best way to grow, especially if Jamie was leaving, would be to get bought by a bigger, more established company. We knew nothing about what it meant to sell a business, which was probably a good thing, because if we'd known how hard it was supposed to be, maybe we would have gotten scared off. But, then again, we had known nothing about what it meant to start a business and we figured that out, so we took the same approach and called in reinforcements.

To sell a business, a company has to create an offering book, which gives potential buyers the preliminary information they need to consider a purchase. It includes things like a business plan, an estimation of what your business is worth, a list of your competitors, and what assets you have in your business. (All questions we'd never thought about until deciding to sell.) My best friend at the time made us an epic offering book as a fortieth birthday present for me. A friend of Jamie's blasted out our information to the Young Presidents' Organization, which he belonged to. To be a member of this organization I think you had to be under forty and the president of a company that was worth at least $10 million. By the grace of God, that email brought us to the attention of Todd and Kim Ferrier, two absolutely fantastic people and the owners of Lifeguard Press, the Kentucky-based company that ended up buying ban.do in 2012. By the time we connected with Todd and Kim, Jamie and I had already met with a few prospective buyers who were just not right. These two, on the other hand, were the perfect fit, and I was sure of it the moment they showed up for our meeting dressed like they were going to a casual brunch rather than a stockholders' meeting. And they had the laid-back attitude to match. They were Southern and reminded me of everyone I loved in college, so I immediately felt as if I was among friends. Todd and Kim smile a lot, laugh a lot, and are also supersmart and willing to take risks, including buying a company like ban.do. Among a million other things, I have learned from Todd and Kim that I don't have to be restricted by the rules or "how things are supposed to be done." (Although, between you and me, I still love a good rule to follow.) They are two of the most generous people I know, and I am eternally grateful to have them in my life.

Aside from making sure that ban.do had the means to stay in business and keep growing, getting bought by Lifeguard Press meant that someone else—someone with real business experience—would be our CEO, and I could be free to focus on the creative side. David Coffey, who I thought was Todd's intern when we first met (sorry, David, you just look so young), was on the Lifeguard Press finance team and eventually became our CEO. On his journey to CEO and my journey to CCO we learned a lot from each other, and in the process became very close friends. On paper we're an unlikely pair—he's a conservative Southern businessman, I'm, well, I'm me—but we balance each other out in a way that ultimately serves the business and the brand well.

Once Lifeguard Press came into the picture, I stayed on as the creative director, Jamie moved to Texas, and the second phase of ban.do's life began.

Chapter 8

I Am Very Busy

For the first couple of years after selling ban.do, we continued to focus on hair accessories but started to dip our toes into some new categories too. And for a small group of creatives with no experience, we did a great job. Eventually, Lifeguard Press encouraged us to do a back-to-school line and said we should include a planner. *You mean, like one of those paper agendas?* I thought. *Do people still use those? Don't they know about Google Cal and smartphones?* Turns out everyone knew about technology and still preferred planners. In fact, those who love planners, really *really* love planners. I couldn't believe it was a thing, but as a lover of paper myself, I was excited to bring something new to the planner market. Ali, our new graphic designer at the time (she's creative director now—good job, Ali), and I spent a ton of time studying the planners currently on the market because I was dead-set on doing something different. Ali was and is always game to roll up her sleeves and figure it out. She quickly became an incredibly important part of our team, and, well, I love her a lot and wish I could claim her as my own, but HR told me that was inappropriate. So anyway, we wanted our planner to feel really personal, like a friend rather than a simple, energy-less book. In order to make that happen, we added in handwritten compliments, insisted on pages of hand-drawn stickers, and used our limited illustration skills along with artwork created by some good friends. We ended up using some of that original art for month openers that were each very different but all bright and colorful, with phrases that encouraged optimism or at least a good laugh. This endeavor would be the birth of our artist collaborations, which have been a major part of our business ever since.

We knew the covers of these planners would be really important, so we spent a ton of time searching for inspiration, doodling pattern ideas on white printer paper, and thinking of phrases that would resonate, although back then we probably called them "fun phrases"—while the concept of emotional resonance was in us, we hadn't totally articulated it yet. I had recently seen a picture of a girl lying on a beach towel (I think it was a beach towel, maybe it was a blanket) that had "BUSY" written on it. I remember being intrigued by the contradiction of her mood and the word. It occurred to me that maybe we should put the phrase "I Am Very Busy" on one of our planners. I liked the humor of it—declaring how busy you are is amusingly self-important—but I also figured if you were buying a planner you must actually feel like you're busy. And you probably *are* busy. Very busy, in fact. Well, that phrase was well-received, to put it mildly, and was our top-selling planner cover for many years. Today, using language that evokes emotional resonance has become a cornerstone of our business. Once, during a product development meeting, one of the guys on our team said to me, "Jen, words don't sell." Turns out he was wrong.

In every cover meeting for years after that planner launched, someone would ask, "Do we have to do IAVB again?" (Nothing says "I work in business" more than an acronym.) And sales would answer with an unwavering YES. And they were right, because it always sold. (This is where the sales team rips out this page and frames it with a note memorializing the one time I admitted they were right.) But over time I got sick of the phrase. First, because as a creative it's almost my job to get bored of ideas and think of new ones, and it's also really normal to reject your work once it comes to fruition. After all, by the time a ban.do product is for sale, I've been looking at it and discussing it and strategizing around it for a full year. By then, the excitement has worn off and there's been too much time to second-guess. Plus, what creatives like to do is create, so by the time an idea of mine is out in the world, I'm focused on the next big thing. All that said, I also developed a sense of guilt around IAVB. As we sold hundreds of thousands of those planners, I began to understand the toxicity in glamorizing busyness, and I recognized my role in that, and it didn't feel good.

And it wasn't just on the planner—I was doing it in my personal life. Like so many other founders and entrepreneurs, I was flaunting my busyness like it was a designer dress I got on clearance. A badge of honor. A sign of success and importance. And in many ways it was, but there are real downsides to being that busy, and those were not talked about, at least not publicly. I don't know that I even understood those downsides initially. It was as if all the female founders that I knew, and considered good friends and a formidable support system, were in a trance. And a friendly, yet potentially detrimental, competition. The busier you were, the more important you were. Or so it felt. The grind became more of a test of will than skill. "I work for fourteen hours a day. I only sleep two hours," we'd say. It was a point of both pride and status. We were glamorizing success in a way that was unhealthy but also deceptive. The lie I was telling myself was that I wasn't a success unless I was constantly in demand, rich, glamorous, and profitable. I've come to find out that success has nothing to do with any of this. Being busy all the time is bullshit, dangerous bullshit. I know I said it twice, but that's how strongly I feel about this. Sue me. But don't sue me, thanks.

From the outside looking in, I imagine that my professional story—founding a company, selling it after only a few years, staying on as the creative lead, and helping to build it into a beloved brand—seems pretty glamorous. Both the news media and social media have glorified the hustle (and the resulting success, as if that's always a guarantee) in ways that make most of us feel like we're failing, even when we're not. If what we're seeing in our feeds is to be believed, success is easy to come by and the hustle is exhilarating, problem-free, and peppered with some really nice vacations.

The reality is that we see a cropped image of success, and the part that gets cropped out is actually the most interesting, it's just not that cute. Every now and then an influential founder or business owner might offer a peek at their own challenges, but what we see is a drop in the bucket compared to the actual number of obstacles they've had to face. Challenges pop up every day, every hour, every minute. There are so many, in fact, that it's a wonder anyone would ever knowingly try to succeed in business. I want to be sure you're aware of this, so when you read this book and decide, "Fuck it, I'm still going to try," I can at least know that I warned you. (Side note: Before ban.do, everyone I spoke to about business told me it was incredibly hard and basically impossible, and I smiled at them with a big toothy grin and walked away thinking, *Not for me it won't be!* And let me tell you, they were right, except for the impossible part.)

Building a business is scary and uncertain, and on a good day it makes you feel like simultaneously throwing up, crying, and laughing, like the day I got that Anthropologie call I mentioned. On a bad day, it just makes you feel like throwing up and crying, like when you accidentally throw out two thousand dollars' worth of Czech crystal headbands and by the time you realize your mistake the trash has already been hauled away. This is especially true for those of us who created monster jobs for ourselves with zero actual experience. It makes you feel like quitting, even if you're not a "quitter." And yes, sure, it is fun and incredibly rewarding, but you sacrifice a lot, you fail a lot, you feel lost a lot, and you don't get many vacations (at least not without your laptop). There is a very real risk of losing yourself, your health, and your life outside of work if you aren't careful.

I've had ban.do for over eleven years, so I'm not saying the pursuit of starting and growing a company isn't worth it, because it's incredibly exciting to watch an idea you had become something that creates jobs and encourages joy in the world, but I had to learn the (very, very) hard way that working around the clock and focusing solely on your company is more about avoidance, denial, and perfectionism than it is about success.

Once we sold ban.do, we experienced very slow, but very exciting growth. We finally got to move out of our tiny office on Beverly into a small, but not tiny, house off

Sunset, across the street from the Chateau Marmont. We had made it. There were five of us when we first moved in, and we fit perfectly into the one-thousand-square-foot house that we dubbed "the Party House." My good friend Emily Henderson helped us design an office that expressed our aesthetic, which included a wall of disco balls and colored gels over most of the windows. In the end those gels really fucked our ability to properly assess Pantone colors, but, hey, another lesson learned! We settled into our vintage blush-velvet-covered office chairs, and even though they squeaked a little, we didn't mind. There was always confetti on the floor from a photo shoot or a Party House event. Our business grew, wholesale started taking off, and suddenly we needed to add more employees. Over the next year and a half, slowly and methodically, we grew our team from five to ten, and the house became so full of desks you could barely walk through it. But at least we had that wall of disco balls, ya know?

Once again, the time was upon us to find a bigger space, and this time we knew we had to plan for more growth. After looking for a couple of months we found an amazing loft-style office space in Hollywood on the third floor of a three-story building. I deemed it "the Penthouse" because even if the building was small, we were at the top. On the day we took the team over to check out the space, everyone was in awe of how big it was. We popped some champagne and toasted to our successes—past, present, and future. Once again, we had made it.

Even with the ten of us and our desks and chairs and bookcases and storage units, the office still felt huge. It reminded me of an old roller-skating rink, and so I bought some roller skates and zipped around the office on wheels. On Fridays I would put on my skates and push around the mail cart, which I loaded with wine spritzers, gleefully shouting, "TGIF, motherfuckers!"

The company continued to do well and had a lot of financial growth, so we started hiring more people and, at least at first, I felt really powerful and successful. "Growth" is a big, important word in the start-up community, and the ability to say, "I am so busy with all this growth" made me feel like a straight-up mogul. I only wish I was better at smoking cigars.

Because I had been in styling, an industry that doesn't follow a set schedule but is always on, I was used to feeling like everything was go-go-go. But back then it was fueled less by wanting to feel important or successful and more about striving to be the best at what I did, and never quite feeling like enough. I would shop all day and night preparing for a job, with very little sleep, just to make sure I had done everything in my power to have as many options as I could and avert failure in any way, shape, or form. I must not have fully trusted myself, and I certainly didn't trust anyone else, so delegating work did not seem like an option.

The feeling of busyness that hit once we started hiring more people and growing as a company was different from what I felt as a stylist, and more extreme even than what I felt when we first launched ban.do. Before we sold, I was spending my days at the office holding a hot-glue gun in one hand and my cell phone in the other, always sitting in front of an open laptop. I would only close it to drive home, and even then, the ride was long enough that sometimes I would pop it open at stoplights to jot down thoughts and finish emails, arriving home after dinner only to open it back up and get back to work. Andrew, as you could imagine, wasn't thrilled with this routine, and with good reason, since losing your wife to a hot-glue gun and a laptop is disheartening.

All of these behaviors only heightened after we moved into the Penthouse. Over the course of maybe eight months, our sales grew so much that we felt like we needed the team to grow alongside it. We went from a team of ten to a team of forty, and that made me feel so successful and proud that I wanted to tattoo the number on my forehead.

As it turned out, growing that quickly was a mistake dressed up to look like success, which in my experience is a pretty common masquerade. I didn't consider for a split second that the growth would amount to anything other than an even larger group of people who would willingly throw their bodies in front of a moving train for ban.do while also not complaining about working some nights and weekends. That was not the case, and the energy in the office started shifting. It didn't feel like the welcoming, intimate company I had started. Suddenly there were a bunch of strangers in the office, some of whom were great—like really, really great—but others just weren't. Maybe they didn't like the job, maybe they were unhappy outside of work, or maybe they just weren't the right fit for ban.do. Or maybe we didn't make it easy for newcomers to settle in, especially those newcomers who wouldn't throw themselves in front of a train for the company on their first day. Probably a combination of all four.

Because the group of the earliest employees, myself included, had no outside experience, when we got the opportunity to expand our team we thought without a doubt that we should hire people with many years of experience under their belts. It's what an *established* company would do. But experience in corporate America and experience at ban.do were two different things, because ban.do was a very small business and you couldn't be siloed in your role and you had to be adaptable and shit went wrong all the time because we were still figuring everything out—and we are still figuring it out. A lot of these new hires came with conviction and baggage and specific ideas of how we should be doing any number of things, and so we did a lot of conforming during that time, because I thought that people who'd worked at successful companies must know better than me, even though ban.do was in my DNA. I had lost touch with the fact that we'd succeeded thus far on innovative ideas and gut reactions rather than experience, and forgetting that important fact was a big mistake.

Those of us who'd been at the company since the beginning, the ones throwing ourselves in front of moving trains for it, took ban.do incredibly personally, and with this rapidly expanding workforce we now felt like we worked at a stereotypical company with office rumors and people shutting down their computers at 6:00 p.m. on the dot. The first time I saw that happen I thought, *What the fuck is she doing? Wait, is she leaving? Right at six?*

I'm going to write her name down on a piece of paper, and I don't know why I'm going to write her name down on a piece of paper, but it seems like the right thing to do in this situation. It happened more and more, and I'd watch them leave and think, *Is this just a job to them?* I know now that that's actually a healthy boundary, but it felt criminal at the time. It was like I was being forced to share custody of my baby with a bunch of strangers who didn't love it nearly enough.

Of course, it wasn't just the growing team that felt foreign to me. Far more difficult was the fact that I was supposed to lead them even though I had no experience managing a team of that size. I didn't know how to properly communicate my creative direction, since I had been working with people who were so plugged in to me and ban.do that they could essentially read my mind. I didn't know how to hold people accountable for anything, and I was terrified at the idea of people quitting. Leading out of fear, avoidance, and inexperience is uncomfortable and unsustainable, but amid your many mistakes you will learn a lot. Also, when you're in charge, all eyes are on you. When there were only five of us in a small office, that didn't feel as obvious because it was a very small room and all our desks kind of faced one another, so everyone's eyes were on everyone all the time, and those eyes usually sat right above a nonjudgmental smile. (And a nose. Obviously, we all had noses.) At the Penthouse, it was different. My office, a large glass room I dubbed the Glass Case of Emotion, was at the very far end of the space, so every day I would make the long walk through the office with many more eyes on me, most of which were attached to friendly faces above encouraging smiles (and noses), but some of which felt judgy and triggered my self-deprecating inner dialogue. I wasn't sure what they were thinking, but I could guess: *Oh, she can just waltz in whenever she wants*, which left me feeling guilty. Or *Ooooh, girl—cute outfit*, which made me feel confident. Or *How did a joke like that find success?* which took the *ooooh, girl* confidence and crushed it like a trash compactor. And I'm sure some people had their eyes on me because they were interested in what I was going to say, or looked up to me in some way, but no matter the reason, people were watching me and I could, and still can, feel it. I'm under a microscope, which is especially hard when your words and actions set the tone for the entire office and you're still learning your management style and then you see your own flaws reflected back to you through what becomes acceptable at your workplace.

As ban.do became more successful, the business side became more difficult. There was more money at stake, but there was also more ego. It's rare to hear founders admit the challenges of getting a product right, or reveal how bad it feels when people don't want the item that you thought was going to be a hit, or discuss dealing with the inevitable lawsuits. But let me tell you, those things hurt. They are humbling and embarrassing and discouraging. They make you question your instincts and your worth. Add to that the fact that I was trying to bring humanity to business, which is really hard. That whole idea of *it's not personal, it's just business?* People really believe that. Of course, for me, and I think for most founders who grow big companies out of ideas they hatched in their living room, business *is* personal.

So while I still loved ban.do, I grew to hate going to work. I had a real aversion to it. I remember talking to my 7958ers and saying, "Don't you wish we could go back to being only five people?"

Despite this, I continued to grind. I left home at 7:00 a.m. and stayed at the office until 7:30 p.m. In retrospect, I think I used my "busy" status as an avoidance tactic more than anything—obviously not to avoid work, but to avoid EVERYTHING ELSE. Shortly after we sold ban.do, I went on a vacation and forgot some of my meds, so I skipped a few doses. I seemed okay, so I decided to go off them entirely. I kept waiting for the other shoe to drop—I thought going off the medication I'd been taking so religiously would feel like falling off a cliff and landing in a deep well of despair and darkness. I think I wanted that to happen, to confirm for me that I needed all those drugs. But it wasn't dramatic at all, it was more like going down a hill gradually, so slowly that you barely notice until you look behind you and see how far you've fallen. And so I stayed off the meds, and on the surface, I was okay. I continued to work hard and find success at ban.do, but I was struggling emotionally. I was crying a lot and eating to numb my feelings, and I was so stressed that I developed rashes all over my body and my hair started to fall out. At one point, I went to South Florida to visit my parents and celebrate my birthday. I had also agreed to officiate Christina's wedding. (It was an intimate affair—four of us on the beach—but still I wanted to knock it out of the park.) Vacations during most of my ban.do life usually meant doing work all day, but from a beach or hotel room rather than the office. During this particular trip, the last-minute project that came in had me totally frazzled and I basically went from house to beach to house to pool while glued to my cell phone. I was constantly checking emails and waiting for calls so that I wouldn't hold up the project. I could feel my anxiety building, and I remember going to the beach with my dad and feeling so overwhelmed and anxious and agitated that I actually scared him.

"You're going to trip and break your neck if you don't watch where you're going," he said as I walked to the beach, eyes glued to my phone.

"Everyone is depending on me," I told him, frustrated that he couldn't understand the urgency of the situation. "I can't just sit here and enjoy myself while everything is falling apart."

"But it's your vacation, and I want to talk to you," he said. I can still see the look of concern on his face today as his daughter, who struggled with anxiety and had already had a nervous breakdown in front of him once, started to buckle under the pressure. There was no calming me down, because I denied that I needed help and resisted it when it was offered. Giving creative direction over the phone on a project that you might be unqualified to lead while suffering from depression and severe anxiety almost always results in an anxiety attack, and it certainly did in this instance. Tears. Emotional shutdown. Crying into the phone. It all happened. I pulled it together in time to officiate the wedding, but it was close. I call that level of pulling yourself together "Katy Perrying." In her *Part of Me* documentary, she's devastated because her marriage is failing and she's sobbing just before her concert starts, and then it's time to go onstage and she just wipes her tears and goes out there and kills it!

All of these red flags, and still I was too busy to notice that I needed my meds. I paid no mind to my mental health, unaware that my depressive episodes were happening more and more frequently. Which is probably why Andrew, who was not that busy, could see in me what I could not see in myself. Every now and then he would suggest I go back on my meds, but I didn't want to hear it and I really didn't want to hear it from him. I wasn't doing well, I realize that now, but I was basically in a work trance, which made denying the emotional stuff quite easy.

I reveled in my busyness for a couple of years and was only snapped out of it when I went to a doctor to get blood work done because I was tired and stressed and was convinced I was slowly dying. When my blood work came back "normal and healthy" I was discouraged and confused.

"What do you do for fun?" the doctor asked me during my exam.

Fun? I thought. *Well, I don't think she means drinking, eating, binge-watching* Breaking Bad, *and crying.* I couldn't think of any intentional fun I was having outside of those things.

I stared at her. "I don't understand," I said. I was definitely a bit defensive. "I don't really have time for fun. I'm very busy. I'm trying to run a business, so that takes most of my focus."

She told me I had to build fun into my schedule. Like literally plan a few hours for it in my calendar each week, because, as so many of us know, if it's on the calendar it is to be honored and respected. That's why, in my Google Calendar, every Wednesday from six to nine has been blocked off for "fun" for years. Fun looks different each week—sometimes I go to dinner with a friend, other times I take a class or go shopping or see a movie. Whatever it takes to help me break the work-sleep-work-drink-work-sleep cycle. Next to the cocktail from the psychiatrist that got my drugs right, "fun" has been one of the best meds I've ever been prescribed.

Taking that step back from the office was critical for me. To start, it prevented me from burning out at ban.do. It also helped me empower other people in the company to step up and take on some of the work I had been too scared to relinquish. I don't hate going to work anymore, not at all, because I was able to establish a life outside of it. Which is not to say that ban.do will ever be "just a job" for me, but I am able to see that my life is more than the company I founded. Stepping back also debunked a myth I'd created for myself, which was that if I stopped grinding, even for just a bit, everything would fall apart. It's a common fallacy that founders tell themselves, but it's just not the case.

There are still parts of business I don't like, but I do love the amount of people you can affect and connect with in a positive way. There's a lot to be gained if you can avoid falling into some of the traps that I did. But that's easier said than done. I was recently with a friend at an event for female founders and there was a young woman in attendance, Ivy League educated, who'd just gotten all this venture capital funding and she was so pridefully busy and also so clearly overwhelmed and talking so fast . . . it felt almost drug-induced. When she left, my friend and I looked at each other and were like, "That doesn't seem healthy." I'm glad I can see that now, and I want to spare others the heartache and health hazard.

If I've scared you a bit, if I've made you think twice about whether business is for you, then I've done my job.

If you're still interested and feeling up to the challenge, here's my advice to all aspiring entrepreneurs:

First, remember that the work is never done. There is always more to do. As Laurel once told me, "You'll die trying to get to the end of the list." Second, once you have your business, decide if growth is really what you want, because growth is not the end-all be-all, and it absolutely should not be the only measure of success. I think there's something appealing about sustainability in business, where you have a small business that you don't need to be a medium or large business. You like the way it runs. You have one or two or five employees. Everyone feels like they're paid well and treated well, and you're making a profit and living the life you want and earning the money you need. These days, the way businesses are in the spotlight—especially female-run companies—the question is always "How big can you get?" And that's really, really hard, especially since most businesses do not end up with all the early employees getting a Porsche and a new house. That is the rare exception. Ban.do is successful, for many reasons, but it's not a billion-dollar company. We grow at a steady pace; we don't take on venture capital; we're profitable each year. It's a slow-and-steady-wins-the-race approach. I rent my home and drive a Volkswagen. It's a great life, but it's not always the one that entrepreneurs envision when they start out. Third, set some boundaries for yourself, so work doesn't swallow you whole. If you crave having a full schedule or get a rush from being busy, first ask yourself why, and then build in other stuff so that you can be busy with more than just work. Schedule a block of fun on Wednesday nights. It's such an important emotional and psychological disconnect, and I'm willing to guarantee right here that it won't change the course of your business. If your company is destined to be successful, you will still be successful even if you carve out time for your personal life.

Because, remember, business doesn't have to equal busyness, and busyness doesn't always equal success. I was very busy long before I was truly successful. In fact, I think a big sign of success is actually *not* being busy, because that means you have learned to delegate in a meaningful way and trust rather than control. It means you have your personal and professional life in perspective. When I go home to Florida these days, my parents are always surprised by my freedom.

"You don't work as much as you used to," they tell me.

"I know," I say. "I moved on up."

Chapter 9

I Cry at Work

Hi, I'm Jen Gotch, and I cry at work.

I also cry in the shower, in my car, on the kitchen floor, in the dressing room at Nordstrom . . . you get the picture.

I'm told that crying at work is controversial in some offices, but since ban.do is my only office experience, outside of that short-lived temp job, I wouldn't really know. At ban.do, emotions are part of our DNA, and I take full credit, or responsibility, for that. When we were a smaller team I would sometimes make the announcement that I was going to cry, and then I'd blink a lot and flail my arms around to add some drama. Now I'm more likely to sit quietly in my office, without causing too much of a disturbance, while also feeling what I need to feel. There are legitimate reasons for me to cry at work: it's my company that I grew from nothing, and I've sacrificed many relationships to nurture it. So when things go wrong there, I'm sad, and when things go right, I'm elated, and both can lead to tears. I often say I have an umbilical cord to the business, so I feel its pain and it feels mine. Also, there are moments when I just hate the pressure and responsibility of being a boss. It's really fucking difficult. Publicly crying may not always be the best way to handle things (or so I've been told by the people forced to witness it), but it can be a necessary release. Plus, they make reliable waterproof mascara now, so you can dry your tears, scoop yourself up off the floor, and get to your next meeting without skipping a beat.

One of my biggest crying-at-work episodes took place, perhaps not surprisingly, the day after Andrew left Los Angeles to move back to the other side of the earth FOREVER. For some reason, I thought it would be best to pretend that I did not just suffer a major loss, so I showered, put on one of my favorite brightly colored floral dresses, did my hair and makeup—I even pulled off the elusive smoky eye—and went to work. I should have taken a day to wallow in my grief, but at some point over the years I had morphed into a soldier who picks herself up, puts on a brave face, and pushes through the pain.

On this particular day, I walked into our office and headed to an e-commerce marketing meeting. I love marketing, but the team in this meeting had a lot of different, oftentimes contrasting, personalities (mine included), so sometimes it could get uncomfortable. To add insult to injury, part of this team was in Kentucky, so the meeting included a conference call. Ugh, the dreaded conference call. They are horrible for pretty much everyone—the timing is always off, the connection always seems as if the phone bill hasn't been paid, and the volume is never loud enough. I'm constantly wondering if the person on the other end of the line likes what I'm saying, and since I can't see their reaction, my brain quickly assures me they do not. Especially when my comments are met by silence, which is often just because someone forgot to unmute their end of the line. Also, hey, I'm trying to talk, but you keep talking, and then you stop talking, and then I stop talking because you were going to let me interrupt and I was going to let you overtalk . . . so yeah, it's frustrating. All that said, the emotions that came over me during this meeting were not commensurate with the experience.

During the call, I ended up in a heated debate with a colleague. I should admit here that for a long time, I would monopolize meetings. I felt like I held the answers to all ban.do-related questions, so why waste time? I think that's part of the founder's mentality. And for a long time I actually did have many of the answers, because there were far fewer questions back then. As the company grew, I came to realize that, first of all, I definitely don't have all the answers. Second of all, the answers I do have aren't necessarily right or wrong, because there could be one hundred right answers at any given time. And third, I'm doing a disservice to the team by solving every problem and answering every question because it doesn't empower them, it keeps them down. They don't have the opportunity to be right or wrong, both of which would teach them something, and it encourages complacency, because if Jen has all the answers, why even try? Still, sometimes my ego gets the better of me, and since I was feeling especially depleted that day, I wasn't exactly making the best choices. Which is how I ended up in a passionate dispute about the critical question of whether an email subject line should read, "Hey, girl, we're having a sale," or "Sale sale sale." (I can't even remember which side of the argument I was on, which should tell you everything you need to know about how clearly I was thinking that day.)

Emotionally, I was hanging on by a thread. I was also in complete denial. I had convinced myself that I was strong and could definitely go to work, because I'd been mourning the loss of my marriage for the past few years, while it was deteriorating. Plus, after dropping Andrew off at the airport the night before, I'd stopped at 7-Eleven and bought one Kit Kat, two packs of Hostess cupcakes, and a Chipwich, and I ate all of them while weeping on my couch in front of an old episode of *The Office.* I figured I'd done all my grieving. Of course, I was wrong, and sometime during that debate I was triggered, and, seemingly out of nowhere, I burst into tears. Literally. Tears were jutting out of my eyes as if they were being shot from a water gun. Salty clear bullets were coming hard and fast, and people ducked for cover to avoid getting drenched.

Thankfully, my friend Kelly, part of the OG ban.do crew and also one of my true ride-or-dies, had been watching me closely during this meeting. She knew what was going on in my personal life, so I think she had an eye on me because she was sensitive to the fact that I could break at any moment. When I finally did, she quickly and quietly got up from her seat, took my hand, and led me out into the stairwell so I could cry in a slightly more private area of the office.

Let me stop here for a second. Why don't we have crying rooms? Not just in offices but, like, everywhere. Sure, there are restrooms and dressing rooms, both of which I've used as crying rooms when necessary, but what about comfortable, dimly lit, soundproof rooms scattered throughout major cities, shopping malls, and workplaces? How great would that be? I imagine something that's part spa, part boutique hotel. Shag rugs, delicious-smelling candles, and a really nice piece of art. Or maybe the entire floor is a cloud of a mattress with comfortable blankets. Heated blankets, weighted blankets! And flowers—gardenias. And soft music that you can turn off if you crave silence. And then there would be a door that looks like a closet, but it's not actually a closet, it's just a door that, if you open it, has a person waiting behind it. A stranger, but a safe, welcoming stranger who is really good at listening and is ready with as many hugs as you need. I think I just came up with my next business. By the time this book is published, mark my words, ban.do will have a crying room. Not sure about the door to the hugger just yet, but I'll keep you posted.

Back then, ban.do did not have a crying room, so, as is the case in most offices, our crying was relegated to stockrooms, bathrooms, or the stairwell. Kelly sat beside me in silence as I hid my face in my hands and tried to wipe away the tears and pull myself together. I heard a few coworkers walk by, but I was too embarrassed to look up.

After a few minutes, when I had calmed down and was a bit easier to rationalize with, Kelly put her hand on my knee, looked resolutely into my eyes, and said, "I really think you need to go home." She was right, and I did.

It was a dramatic episode, and I think there are probably levels of crying, and mine had perhaps surpassed the level that is appropriate at work, even at ban.do. Although I clearly advocate for emotions in the workplace, I also think it's important that everyone, both employees and employers, are responsible with their emotions so that their expression doesn't alienate people or replace productivity. In the case of my minor meltdown, it at least helped to establish the office as a safe place for all employees to display emotion, so I can't say I entirely regret it.

Although this was my most memorable office cry, it wasn't my first and certainly wasn't my last. I've cried at almost every job I've ever had, often due to various horrible bosses, and those instances ended up being good lessons for me when I became a boss myself. I cried in the bathroom of the nursing home where I was a waitress at age thirteen, because the girls who were in charge hated me and made sure to let me know. I cried in the bathroom of a café where I worked in college, because the owner cornered me and tried to kiss me, and it made me feel unsafe. I cried while styling a shoot for *Bon Appétit* magazine in Santa Barbara, when the photographer didn't like the props I brought and, in front of the entire crew, yelled, "Is there even a brain inside your head?" For that cry, I found the laundry room of the house where we were shooting and pretended to be ironing some linen napkins while sobbing uncontrollably. Eventually we resolved it, and this photographer went on to hire me many more times. Variations on this story happened on a couple of different shoots, with photographers who didn't believe in me—or themselves—and let me know as much. I've been shooed out of meetings with that flippy hand gesture indicating that "Um, we don't need you anymore, goodbye." I've had bosses take credit for my work, right in front of me, or rescind their offers to pay me once the job was done.

There were some good bosses too, who modeled for me what it looked like to embrace emotions in a positive way. A stylist I ended up assisting for many years was incredibly kind and generous with her time and money, and always recognized me for my contributions to the job. An art director I worked for taught me about creating on demand and making the most of any situation. I watched both of these women emote at work. Maybe it was crying in the prop closet or being unable to hide their frustration, but it was always a sign that they were plugged into their passion.

These interactions with bosses, both good and bad, helped shape my management style and influenced the type of work environment I would go on to create at ban.do. As someone running a company, I never want to *make* anyone cry in the office. I make a point to avoid doing anything that might put anyone in that position. But I have also come to learn that you can't protect people from their emotions. You can create an office culture that is kind and nurturing, but feelings are feelings and being human can be very painful at very inconvenient times.

In the early days of ban.do, while I was still working to get my own mental health in check, I was definitely guilty of oversharing and bringing my emotional baggage into the workplace. Our office was small, and I would sit down at the giant conference table and spill my feelings all over the place for other people to clean up. Some people don't mind that, but plenty would prefer not to have to pick up after your emotional mess, especially if they didn't even ask how you were doing. Jamie, who was much better at setting boundaries than I, once told me that I had to be better about not bringing my personal problems to work, because it was a burden and stressor that she didn't want to be responsible for. When she said it I kind of wanted to spit in her eye, but what she was saying was totally fair. It just didn't feel fair at the time. And that's why I called her a bitch under my breath, and for that I am sorry.

I know now that there are healthy ways to show emotion in the office, and less healthy ways. Today I try hard to strike a balance between displaying emotion and unloading on people. I think my colleagues would say I've been successful in that regard, and so I've turned that supposed "weakness"—basically, having the audacity to be human in the workplace—into a strength, because I've established a company that allows employees to safely feel their feelings.

Frankly, the concept of not bringing emotions to work seems foreign to me. For those of us in the creative world especially, tapping into emotion is part of what we do. How can we identify the products that will inspire happiness if we aren't allowed to feel the full spectrum of feelings? Sometimes the job requires accessing emotions that may not have traditionally been work appropriate, but at ban.do we're changing that. Empathy is at the core of our company culture. As a result, there are tears, they are plenty, and they often end up in my office. I'm happy they do.

People cry at work for all sorts of reasons. They cry because they have stress at home, or they have health issues, family issues, work stress, mental health issues. They're overwhelmed, they're sad, they're happy, they're excited, they're uncertain. They just lost their job. They were just offered a promotion. Or maybe there was just a really fucking cute puppy in the office. I feel like at least three people cried when Waffles the puppy came into ban.do.

Here is my rallying cry for bosses: Treat your team with respect and constantly challenge yourself to build your own self-awareness and emotional intelligence. Permit people to be human. And behave like a human yourself. There should still be rules and regulations and boundaries—displays of emotion should always be handled responsibly, so that employees feel safe and respected, and bosses aren't putting workers in uncomfortable situations—but making people feel seen and heard and ultimately understood is something the modern workplace should continue to emphasize and prioritize. Do not be emotionally abusive, and do not use people's emotions against them, especially if they have come to you to discuss them, which is a really brave thing to do.

And if you're a boss who isn't personally comfortable with tears? Well, tell your employees it's okay to feel their feelings, then encourage them to head to the Crying Room™.

Chapter 10

My First Husband

When Andrew and I got married, the one thing I knew for sure is that we would never, ever, ever get divorced.

Then, eleven years later, we got divorced.

The end.

Just kidding. I've spent a lot of time thinking about marriage and divorce since our marriage ended, so of course I have plenty more to say. And I'm going to tell you what I wish I'd known and what I learned, because it might give you insight into some of your relationships. It certainly would have saved me and Andrew a ton of pain and wasted time, and although I don't encourage looking back with regret, I do think hindsight, with a bit of introspection, can be incredibly valuable.

My biggest revelation about my marriage starts with a conversation I had with my psychiatrist only recently. As I've mentioned, when you have bipolar disorder, your meds are managed by a psychiatrist who needs to speak to you at least quarterly for check-ins. They ask you a list of questions in order to assess your mental well-being and troubleshoot problems, and one of those questions is "How is your judgment?" Judgment is a point of focus with bipolar, because lapses in judgment can sometimes be caused by changes in brain chemistry, which is managed by your meds. Sometimes they are just caused by spontaneity. Some of my personal lapses in judgment, none of which I regret, have been moving across the country with no job, starting a company without a plan, buying a house with no savings, and deciding to get married after knowing someone for only a week.

Those decisions all led me to where I am today, and I really like where I am, so I have to imagine that, in some way, they were good choices—strange and impulsive at times, but good. I'm not saying that all lapses in judgment are caused by mental illness—if you've made it this far in this book, you know there are lots of factors that contribute to who we are and how we make decisions.

So anyway, I was on the phone with my psychiatrist, and he asked me about my judgment. His question struck me because I'd been feeling like my judgment in general was a little compromised.

"Well, actually, I think my judgment is a little off," I said.

"Oh, okay. How so?" he asked. "Are you feeling like your mood is unstable? Are you having any other bipolar symptoms?"

"Nope, just the judgment, and I don't feel like it's an episode. If I'm being honest, I think I accidentally fell in love." I'd recently started dating someone new, and I felt like my penchant for falling hard and fast was flaring up again.

"Infatuation lasts from six to eighteen months," he said.

"*Whhhaaaat?*" I was floored.

"Infatuation lasts for six to eighteen months," he repeated, as if my *whhhaaaat?* meant "Can you please say the same thing again?" not "What the fuck are you talking about?" Then he went on to explain that infatuation is essentially a chemical reaction necessary to propagate the species, so it happens to all of us. It is a huge lapse in judgment that can warp your perspective on both yourself and the object of your affection, and prompt you to make decisions based on fantasy.

"This, Dr. Engel, is information I could have used yesterday," I said, half joking but totally not joking.

My head was spinning. He had basically described exactly how I was feeling in this new relationship, which felt like a relief but also like "Oh, fuck, I'm falling in love," and that both excited and terrified me. But my thoughts very quickly shifted to Andrew, and I started mentally calculating the timeline of our relationship. When we finished our call, my psychiatrist wished me luck with my current situation and confirmed we would speak in a few months. I thanked him profusely, because although my head was spinning, he had just given me total clarity on a major reason my marriage didn't work out.

Andrew and I had a whirlwind romance. It was a fantasy that I wholeheartedly believed I had earned. I was the last of my friends to get married, and I felt like our love story was my reward for being patient and feeling genuinely happy as I watched everyone around me fall in love, get married, buy houses, and start families while I remained very, very single. The fact that I was alone actually didn't bother me . . . until it did. And then it really bothered me. And then, as I've told you, I asked the universe to bring me love, and, like magic, Andrew appeared.

Once Andrew and I decided to get married—after that one week of knowing each other—I called my parents to tell them the good news: I was heading to Vegas with a stranger and the next time we spoke, I'd have a husband. I think they were so relieved that I'd no longer be alone that they were actually excited rather than horrified, as some parents might have been at such a hasty major life decision. Or maybe they were just in shock, but I took it as a sign that this was, in fact, an excellent idea. We ended up prolonging the courtship, and so we spent the next nine months going back and forth, visiting each other in Melbourne or LA, so we were more or less on vacation whenever we were together. And we all know, because we have seen *The Bachelor*, that how you act on vacation, while infatuated, is not indicative of how you act in real life.

It's not that our relationship wasn't real. I did love him, and he loved me. We were just very different people, though I thought where we overlapped made sense and where we didn't seemed interesting. He was kind and handsome and a great kisser. We were a socioeconomic mismatch—he was a mechanic and aspiring photographer,

I was a working stylist who would often take my car to a mechanic—but that made me feel like I was taking a risk, and I was in the mood to take some very big risks. He wasn't the person my parents expected me to end up with, and in many ways I think that was part of the draw, I was daring to be different. And on a personal level, we connected. I felt really comfortable with Andrew from the moment I met him, and that was a new feeling for me. I'm sure a lot of that had to do with the fact that I was in a better place. I had a career, I had friends, I went to therapy, I was managing my mental health—I was more myself than I had ever been. And for the record, I'm kind of weird—not in a good or bad way, just in more of a not-your-average-girl kind of way. (You probably know that by now.) In my experience, that complexity can be quite off-putting for men, so I always had a soft spot for the ones who embraced it rather than making me feel like my quirks weren't appealing. Andrew was different from most men I knew and different from what I thought was "my type." While most guys I'd encountered in LA wanted to model or act and wouldn't dare sully their exterior, he had rough hands from building stuff and taking stuff apart. He didn't know what was "cool" and he didn't care either. And he operated without pretense in a town where pretension is pervasive. Andrew was who he was, take it or leave it. Plus there was some mystery to him, at least at first—that whole being-from-another-hemisphere thing, I guess. His stories and knowledge intrigued me, his accent was really fun to listen to, and he didn't even flinch when I told him that I suffered from bipolar disorder, which, if you have mental illness and have ever had to tell someone you really like about it, you know how scary that can be. He was, and continued to be throughout our entire marriage, a total champion when it came to helping me navigate my mental health.

I'll admit there were times, before we were married, when I had doubts. Sometimes it was just a feeling in my gut, my intuition trying to steer me in the right direction, but my mind was made up, so I dismissed those whispers. Every now and then Andrew said or did something that probably indicated future problems, but again, I didn't pay them much attention. A friend once told me that everything you need to know about the person you're dating, they tell you early on. Sometimes they tell you through their actions, other times they actually just tell you. But we usually don't accept the messages, because we're under a love spell and these truths don't fit into the fantasy we've created. Hold on to that insight for a second. No, really, hold on to it, because it might actually save you a lot of heartache.

A year and a half into our relationship, and about six months into our marriage, Andrew and I were still high on the fumes of love, living out the fantasy of married life. We outfitted our kitchen with new plates and flatware, and we even bought a wok. We celebrated holidays together for the first time. Halloween was especially fun. They don't celebrate it in Australia, so I turned our apartment into a haunted house and scared the shit out of him.

Then, one day, the spell lifted, not unlike Cinderella's clock striking midnight. I woke up one morning and looked over at Andrew, and that intense feeling of admiration and desire had evaporated. It was shocking. Even now, almost fourteen years later, I can remember the morning so vividly that I can still smell the laundry detergent we used on our sheets. I immediately started crying, and Andrew, who was such a sweet, caring husband especially when it came to my emotions and my overall mental health, asked what was wrong.

And I told him.

Something is happening, I said frantically. *Things are changing. My feelings are changing, and it seems like the fairy tale ended with no warning. I don't want to lose it and I deserved it and I waited and I was so patient and it can't leave, I don't know what I would do.* (What I didn't say, but was thinking, was that I also didn't know what I would do if this was my new normal—our new normal.) Andrew put his hand on my leg and assured me it was okay and that it was totally normal for feelings to change and evolve. *The fantasy of the honeymoon phase can't last forever,* he told me.

It was one of the wisest things he ever said. I don't know if I gave him credit for that. How did he know?

He was right, but I wasn't hearing it. Honestly, sometimes I could be a real dick. I wouldn't listen to his advice, especially when it was counter to what I wanted to hear. My answer throughout most of our marriage was no. Just in case you were feeling sorry for me, don't. I was not always an ideal partner.

After that morning I cried every day for a week straight. I couldn't believe what was happening. I couldn't believe I had been tricked and trapped (not by Andrew, but by my brain) and that I wasn't actually getting a fairy tale. The spell had lifted, and now I was getting what all of us get: a relationship that is grounded in reality, with real problems, and real stress. It also had love and admiration, but without trust and respect those feelings become inconsistent, fleeting and, if you're not careful (and we weren't), they go away altogether.

Andrew and I tried really hard to keep our marriage afloat, but things just got worse over time. At first, Andrew couldn't work because of green card and work permit issues. He didn't love living in Los Angeles, which was a far cry from Melbourne, and so he never fully settled in. I had a lot of guilt about that, since he moved to the States to be with me. He left a safe environment where he knew his way around and had tons of friends and close family and a favorite fish-and-chips shop for a city that felt less safe and where he was constantly lost. And I mean lost literally, because LA freeways and the signage they come with are the worst, but he was also lost emotionally. Andrew had come to the US with dreams of becoming a commercial car photographer, but neither of us knew what a tough industry that was to break into. He had a background in photography, which he taught at the University of Melbourne, but car photography was his dream. When he finally was able to work, he managed to get a job shooting for a car magazine, but it kind of went sideways, which upended his confidence, and he didn't get many photography jobs after that. He was clearly, and with good reason, feeling defeated and unhappy and insecure.

I, on the other hand, was thriving. I was at the height of my styling career when I met Andrew and I eventually parlayed that into ban.do, which, in my mind, delivered the crushing blow to our marriage, although we didn't realize it at the time.

Success is hard on a relationship. There are wonderful aspects to it, of course, but it can be lonely, especially when the people closest to you are not experiencing their own success. It can cause jealousy and insecurity, and I think that is only heightened when it's the woman in the relationship who is succeeding. That sounds harsh, but I say it not just based on my own experience but also that of a lot of my friends who've had similar difficulties with their husbands. A woman's success can be incredibly emasculating—a word I learned once I found success. I was grateful that ban.do was thriving, and proud that I was building something and that I was making enough money to afford us a nice life, but it ripped Andrew apart, because although he contributed in many ways, he wasn't able to contribute financially in the way he'd hoped.

I was also so focused on ban.do that I imagine I was very dismissive of Andrew. In fact, I'm 100 percent sure that I was, because I remember being that way and I remember him telling me I was that way, and I remember denying it even though I knew it was true. And that wasn't because I wasn't grateful for him (though I could have been better about expressing that gratitude), but because I was consumed with work. I never did anything intentionally hurtful—and neither did he—but what we each needed from our partners was beginning to evolve. On my end, I needed a partner who I could lean on and who would lean on me. But I didn't understand how much independence some men need, and how they would rather solve things on their own. For years, I thought I was doing Andrew a service when I tried to help him find jobs or network or settle into his new city, but I may have actually been knocking down his confidence. I wanted to discuss my feelings all the time, he definitely did not. Also, he just had bad luck. Like, epically bad luck. Things seemed to continually not go his way—the man had more flat tires than anyone I had ever known, which doesn't seem like that big of a deal, but on the freeways of LA it really is.

Over time, all the ways that we were different started to feel more annoying than interesting, and then more disconcerting than annoying, and then just isolating.

As our relationship progressed, I lost my trust in

Andrew and my respect for him, and perhaps he for me. Without those things love is hard to foster and there is no relationship, but still we tried to fix what was broken between us. If a lot is going right in a relationship, small tweaks can make the connection even stronger. But when things are bad, the small tweaks aren't enough. We tried to spend more time together, connect over common interests, laugh at the same jokes. All things that were—and are—important, but it's trust and respect that create a lifeline for a long-term relationship and help it thrive when the intoxication of that initial deep zombielike love spell wears off. Trust and respect take a long time to build, and they need to be tested and survived over and over again. They are precious, and I didn't treat them that way. Once they're lost they're hard to recover, and Andrew and I realized this too late.

When things first started going bad we fought a lot, really going at it, but then it just stopped. We didn't argue, we just coexisted. There was no passion—and yes, I'm talking about sex.

"It worries me that you don't fight at all," Laurel, my therapist, told me one day. "There's passion in fighting, and the fact that you've given up the fight makes me wonder if this marriage is salvageable."

"I don't know if it is, but I don't want to go back out there," I said. "Dating is the worst, and I don't want to do it, and, anyway, what would we do with our pets?" Yes, you read that right, I wanted to stay married for the sake of the dog.

One day, I opened up Safari on our shared desktop computer and there in the search bar was the phrase "How to get a divorce." I wasn't even mad or upset, just more curious than anything. *Well this is an interesting development*, I thought. *And also, how do you do it?* We both wanted to get divorced, but also we both didn't. For so long I took a high-and-mighty approach to divorce. I thought I was above it, not one of those people who defaulted to breaking up as soon as things got difficult. Any problem could be solved with hard work and persistence, right? (WRONG.) From my vantage point, the vows we took on our wedding day were sacred and binding, and I was loyal and good and would honor that commitment, even if it was going to be an uphill battle. Also, and this is probably obvious to you though I didn't admit it to myself at the time, I was avoiding divorce because I was avoiding the pain and fear that came along with that decision.

We did talk about it sometimes, what it would be like to break up, but I just thought, *I'm not going to pull the trigger, and he's not going to pull the trigger, so we're going to have to figure out how to be married this way.*

What was I so scared of, you ask? At first it was the shame and embarrassment of admitting our relationship wasn't working, and of admitting that deciding to get married after only knowing each other for a week maybe was a mistake after all. I was also legitimately scared of how it would affect our dog. Our fucking dog. If we had kids Andrew would probably still be living here and I definitely wouldn't be writing this book, or at least this chapter.

In the last three years before we separated, what I was most scared of was having to start over in my forties. The thought of dating as a grown-up woman in Los Angeles was unappealing, and I had already done it for like ten years before meeting Andrew and I hated every second of it. Maybe I enjoyed about 240 seconds, actually, but the rest were a total shit show filled with self-doubt, insecurity, isolation, and at least one guy named Herb, so, yeah, I wasn't going back.

I don't know exactly what Andrew's fears were, but I know that he was hurting, and I know he must have been scared of something too, because he stuck it out with me. I do know he felt the same way as I did about divorce and agreed it was a solution for other people, but not us.

So, given my age and my pets and my fears, I was ready to

adjust my expectations about how good and full life could be and instead lock some of my dreams in a box in the attic and never think about them again. That was my solution—cut myself off from my emotions for the next forty years so that I could stay married for my dog. (I get that the dog won't be alive for forty years, but I'm looking into the science of that, and if I find anything out I promise I'll write a book about keeping your beloved pets alive because they are cute and fun to cuddle and enable you to make bad decisions like "stay in a failed marriage for the dog.")

One day, after eleven years of marriage, Andrew made the choice for us. I had been on a weekend getaway with friends and had just returned home, exhausted from a long day of travel. After dumping my luggage at the door, I walked into the living room and found him sitting on the couch, watching an episode of *The Walking Dead*, which we were supposed to watch together. He had one of the strangest looks on his face, and I immediately assumed it was because he was caught watching zombies without me.

"Hey, Jenni. I have something I want to talk to you about," he said.

The words I'd been waiting to hear for years had finally arrived. Our breakthrough. We were going to talk.

"I think we should get a divorce."

My immediate reaction was shock—I knew we'd both considered divorce, but I never thought either of us would actually pursue it—but it was almost immediately followed by relief. It was like I could breathe for just a moment. But then it felt like a piano fell out of the sky and onto my head. It was a strange three seconds.

We had our talk. Andrew finally shared how unhappy he was and that he just didn't know what else to do. I knew it was the right choice, but I was also scared and didn't want him to make any quick decisions. I suggested that he move back to Australia for a few months and get a glimpse of his life there to make sure it was what he wanted. Remember, he wasn't a US citizen, so if he didn't return to the States within three months he would lose his permanent residency. I wanted him to be sure, because I knew if he packed up everything and moved home, and we got a divorce, he couldn't come back.

Andrew took my advice and went home, and I really enjoyed my time alone. I got a glimpse of what my life could be and, honestly, I assumed that he was having a similar experience. In fact, I was quite sure that he wasn't going to return, and that at the end of our trial separation he would tell me he'd given it some thought and he officially wanted a divorce.

Toward the end of his time in Australia, Andrew sent me an email. I opened it knowing this was going to be an email that would determine the rest of my life, so I scrolled very very slowly. The first couple of lines read like an official breakup letter, and as I read them I prepared myself for an emotional nosedive. *Okay, here we go,* I thought. And the next line read, "I've decided I want to come back and work it out."

Huh, I thought. *All right, then.* I was surprised, confused, and strangely hopeful. It sounded like Andrew recognized there were things he needed to change and that he wanted to work on our relationship. It wasn't until years after we were actually divorced that I realized I had a lot to work on as well. But at this point, I just hoped we'd be able to salvage our marriage at least to a place that felt fulfilling, even if it wasn't everything we once dreamed it would be.

So Andrew returned to LA and, to his credit, he really tried. He went to therapy, read books, and tried to take an optimistic approach to all of it. But it was too far gone, he was so numb. We both were, and within a couple of months, we fell back into the old routine, and I went back to accepting that this was how my life was going to be.

A month later, Andrew's dad got a bad case of bronchitis,

and then a couple of days after that he was hospitalized. Andrew and I were worried but not overly concerned. One evening, when we were lying in bed, his mom called. I tried to scoot close to him, so I could hear what she was saying, but her voice was muffled. I could see on Andrew's face that something horrible had happened. He hung up the phone and turned to me. "Dad's got cancer." I sat very still and silent, but my intuition whispered a very straightforward "You're getting divorced." It was one of those lightning-bolt-to-the-head moments that comes without even an ounce of doubt. His family was so tight-knit, and I knew he would move home and want me to come with him, and I knew I wouldn't go. This time I wouldn't resist my gut. After a series of not-so-subtle nudges from the universe, this sign came in and practically pushed me off the bed.

We spent the next three weeks packing Andrew's stuff and tying up loose ends. I was incredibly sad, not because we were getting divorced—I knew that was the right choice for us—but because I was grieving the relationship. And we were still friends. We didn't hate each other. It really was a conscious uncoupling (hey, Gwyneth), and in some ways an amicable divorce is harder because you aren't fueled by rage. This person who had been central to my life for the last twelve years was leaving and moving to another hemisphere. We weren't going to run into each other at the grocery store. We most likely weren't going to see each other ever again.

So, yes, it was super sad, but that felt appropriate for the end of a marriage. It was also freeing. When you're married, your partner's pain is your pain, their suffering is your suffering. But suddenly his suffering wasn't going to be my responsibility anymore. I was going to get another chance. The life I had resigned myself to, because I felt it was the right thing to do and because I felt too weak and too scared to actually make any changes, now held opportunity. I can vividly remember dropping Andrew off at the airport, watching him wave goodbye in my rearview mirror, and driving home. It was as if I was watching myself from outside my body, thinking, *I am driving into the next phase of my life. This is day one. Now I just need to stop and get some Hostess cupcakes and a Kit Kat for the journey.*

In reality, once the dust settled on Andrew's departure, things slowly got very, very dark for me, but I, for one, can only see the light after I've come out of an emotional midnight. I had been so busy dealing with his feelings, making emotional and personal sacrifices to not rock the boat, that I was denying my own suffering, avoiding my own emotional needs or numbing myself to them entirely.

Shoutout to work, shoutout to food, shoutout to booze, shoutout to Netflix. Once Andrew was gone, the floodgates opened. The Christmas after he left, I decided to carry on our annual tradition of the Christmas Day Whiskey Tasting, something I had invented several years earlier. As a Jew with little Christmas experience I was extremely proud of this idea and wanted the tradition to live on. My brother came over, as did Christina and her husband, and I got so drunk that at one point I ended up changing into a Darth Vader costume (don't ask) and insisting that we listen exclusively to the *Star Wars* soundtrack. When we ran out of whiskey I thought it best to pivot to champagne and my highly popular mouth mimosas. (It's a drink with no cup—you just pour equal parts orange juice and champagne in your mouth and then swallow. Very sophisticated.) But when I went to grab the champagne bottle out of the fridge, I dropped it on my foot and broke my toe. My physical run-ins with bottles of alcohol were becoming my patented rock-bottom wake-up call. Shortly afterward, my dad, the podiatrist, confirmed my diagnosis during a very awkward FaceTime in which I was still in costume and basically incoherent. My pain, both physical and emotional, was beginning to bubble up and demand attention.

I was still off my meds, and clearly struggling with both my bipolar disorder and my anxiety along with all the feelings that accompany a divorce. Diving into work helped me avoid a lot of this pain, but the broken toe cracked me open. Literally, sure, but it also slowed me down enough that I could take a close look at my behavior and see very clearly that I needed help.

When things were at their worst in our marriage, I would sometimes look over at Andrew and think, "He's my *first* husband." Turns out I was right. In the end, the divorce was a gift. It was the catalyst for personal growth and healing that stretched far beyond the anguish of a major breakup. I feel lucky that I had the awareness and resilience to face the pain and accept my role in our failed relationship—and believe me it was a starring role. The divorce, although a radical life change that some might view as a failure, was actually the first step in a process that would take me to a far better place. It was without a doubt the ending I needed in order to find a new beginning.

Chapter 11

Hello, Crispy Cereal

Emotional eating, and by that I mean eating not because you're hungry or need nutrients but because you're feeling sad or happy or stressed or celebratory or tired, was modeled for me at a very young age. I didn't recognize it as emotional eating back then, especially since my dad isn't a super outwardly emotional guy, but I used to sit and watch him devour trail mix or cookies completely mindlessly. Oh my God, there was this fruit-and-nut bread that he loved—he'd lay on the couch, a kitchen towel draped over his chest, and he'd meticulously pick out the fruits and the nuts like he was performing surgery. Then he'd eat them, breaking free of his food trance only long enough to get up and throw away the sad pile of bread bits when it got too big for the towel to contain. I'm not even sure he was aware he was doing it, but I definitely internalized early on that food could be used to soothe, numb, punish, or protect, and it didn't take long for me to adopt it as my drug of choice.

In my junior and senior years of college, and in the first few years after graduating, eating became my most reliable coping mechanism. I like to think I earned a black belt in emotional eating, a welcome distraction from the adulthood that I was completely avoiding.

By the time I moved in with my friend Forrest in Atlanta, I had fixated my eating on cereal specifically. Like my father before me, I liked the kind of eating that required high concentration and a sense of monotony. At the time, I was pretty much hibernating in our apartment in order to avoid real life. I couldn't really cook yet, and when you're not leaving the house and there is no Postmates, because it's 1994, cereal it is. Chex or Cheerios, I'm not even sure anymore. Something crispy, without a lot of flavor, because I was mostly in it for the crunch. I would eat the cereal really fast, so that it didn't get soggy, and I found comfort in the repetition of spooning in each mouthful. One afternoon I was eating my cereal and was faced with a decision: finish the bowl or pee. The clock was ticking on sogginess, but I made a run for it. I really had to pee. When I got out of the bathroom, probably sixty seconds later, the bowl was gone. Forrest had taken it, dumped the cereal, and washed and put away the dish all in the time it took me to pee. I thought about murdering her all day.

Forrest was a very neat person, and I was a slob, so I'm sure she just saw the bowl and thought in her sweet, Southern tone that I love so much, *I'm going to kill her—right after I clean up her mess*, but honestly the effect of her rapid cleanliness in that moment felt to me as if someone had flushed my drugs down the toilet, and I was devastated. I'm sure I played it cool, and then went into my room and screamed into a pillow, but the reality was, my cereal was my security blanket and she had messed with it. Between you and me, I probably had two full boxes stowed away in the cabinet, so I eventually forgave her.

I asked Forrest about this recently. She's still a very dear friend, and I was surprised—but glad—to hear that she doesn't even remember it. (Clearly some of my pivotal memories didn't make much of an impression on the people around me. Though it makes sense she wouldn't remember washing a dish, because, knowing Forrest, she's washed millions in her lifetime. I've only had my cereal dumped prematurely once.) The incident made a huge impact on me, probably because I knew, at least deep down, that my reaction was irrational and that something deeper was going on. Cereal probably shouldn't be front and center of anyone's life.

As the years passed and I continued to struggle with my mental health and emotional well-being, I stepped up my game from cereal to the hard stuff, like fast food and bowls of pasta bigger than my head, which made it really easy to put my whole face in there. In retrospect, it's so clear that I was self-medicating. I hadn't yet been properly diagnosed or properly medicated, so I used food to try to feel better. I mean, that feeling you get when a McDonald's french fry hits your lips? I've never done cocaine, but I can't imagine it's much better than that.

When I wasn't eating to numb my pain, I was eating to insulate myself so that I couldn't feel at all. I would pack on weight until I felt unrecognizable, trying to disassociate from my body and punish myself for overeating with more eating. Gaining weight was a way to distance myself from other people too, because I felt repellant, and people pick up on that stuff. That sort of self-inflicted suffering was a constant for me for a long time. It didn't matter that, in reality, I wasn't overweight. I'm a small-boned person, so when I put on twenty pounds, it may look fine to strangers, but I know it's not where my healthy body should be.

I can articulate all this now, but I didn't become conscious of my distorted relationship with food until I started seeing Laurel.

Laurel was very passionate about the mind/body connection, long before mind/body became the widely understood concept it is today. She had a vast and constantly growing knowledge about the interplay between physical and mental health, and she helped me understand that hurting one hurts the other (and helping one helps the other). She taught me that getting to know our bodies, and being able to understand and identify subtle symptoms, becomes an incredible tool to use for our own personal wellness.

I also learned the extent to which what we eat and drink affects not just our bodies but our brains. This was a major eye-opener for me because, until that point, what I knew was that fat made you fat, and that carbs and sugar were the enemy—diet culture had shifted by then to a no-carb obsession—and that too much of any of them would make your jeans tight. I knew that sometimes I got so hungry that I wanted to kill someone, but I had never heard of low blood sugar. I found out about gluten. Fucking gluten. If you told me as a kid that I'd have to stop eating bread in order to feel better because of something called gluten, I would have kicked you in the shins and, with eyes full of tears, asked you where all my peanut butter and jelly was supposed to go.

With Laurel's guidance, I began to change my eating in an attempt to feel better and take some pressure off my beleaguered brain.

For the next decade or so, I vacillated between emotional eating, which was essentially my baseline, and fighting against that with therapy, exercise, and a sensible diet. It was very cyclical. I'd get to my max weight, then decide I was going to diet and work out every day to the point of obsession, then I'd injure myself and fall off the wagon, landing headfirst into a Crunchwrap Supreme.

This pattern was only heightened in my marriage, because one of the few things Andrew and I had in common was emotional eating. And given how many emotions we were dealing with, or actually not dealing with, we spent a lot of time eating. A large ham-and-pineapple pizza and four episodes of *Breaking Bad* are way more fun than actually facing your problems.

In 2016, during the three-week period between deciding on a trial separation and Andrew's actual move to Australia, I remember saying "let's just eat or drink whatever we want for the next three weeks, because it's going to be a really hard time." I didn't want to add guilt about eating to all the other emotions we were struggling with, and so we ate and we drank, and it was actually really fun. But in that three weeks (and really, the year and a half before that, when things were especially bad between us, and also the year and a half after we decided to get divorced, when I was recovering from our split), I gained a lot of weight and again found myself in the body of someone I didn't recognize. For a while, I subsisted largely on Tate's chocolate chip cookies, which I still love to this day, and McDonald's ice cream sundaes, which I also still love to this day. At work I shifted from wearing cute dresses to showing up in UGG boots and pajamas—turns out tears aren't the only way to bring emotions to the workplace. And sure, I was still succeeding professionally at ban.do, but in my personal life I was feeling lost, sad, and numb, and there's no way that wasn't going to seep through somehow.

Eventually, after Andrew and I broke up for good, the fog started to clear. I finally had the headspace to think about only myself, which I hadn't done in more than a decade because I'd been so focused on my marriage and on Andrew's happiness. During that time I realized that *man,*

I don't like how I feel in my body or my clothes, and I'm relying on food for emotional nourishment. It was time to make a change, this time for the long haul.

After the rock-bottom episode when I broke my toe at the whiskey-tasting party, I decided it was time to go back on my meds. Not only was it clear that my bipolar disorder was acting up, but my ADD was making it really hard for me to get work done, and I was really invested in getting work done. I had been off the meds for some time, so when I approached my psychiatrist about starting again, he wanted me to start slow and stairstep up to a therapeutic dose, which would take some time. I was eager for more instant relief, and I knew that focusing on a healthy diet and exercise plan could give me that. I cut down on carbs and increased my intake of protein and veggies. After about a week, I began to feel better. Between the new eating habits and the gradual stairstepping of my meds, after a few months, I stabilized and was able to tackle the real emotional issues in a more meaningful way.

Shortly after shifting into these healthier nutrition habits, I was getting my hair done and talking to my friend Leonie, who has highlighted my hair forever, when she mentioned that she had recently gone to a food therapist. I'd never even heard of such a thing, but I'm generally very aware of when these gifts of information are given to me. I don't really believe in coincidences.

"A food therapist? OMG, so LA," I said. But honestly, I was curious. "What does that even mean?"

"She's just like a regular therapist, except she deals specifically with people's issues around food."

Umm, yeah, sign me up. I got the therapist's number on the spot and within a week I had an appointment. She was friendly, with a peaceful disposition, and she was easy to open up to. I could tell immediately that she knew what she was talking about and also that she had a very holistic approach to relationships with food. I immediately trusted her, which is saying something, because with the amount of therapy I've had in my life, I can be very skeptical of therapists. I am now going to tell you everything she told me, which will save you approximately 250 bucks, so maybe think of donating some of that to a charity of your choice.

Before I lay it on you, I should point out that I'm not saying the tools and information she gave me were revolutionary. They weren't necessarily ideas I hadn't heard before, but something about the way she phrased them just clicked with me. Plus, with a lifetime of problem-solving under my belt, I've come to find that solutions tend to be a lot simpler than we want or expect them to be. It started with the concept that the key to emotional eating—or just healthy eating habits in general—is to not get too hungry.

See what I mean? So simple. First of all, if you get too hungry, you might become a raging bitch. Second of all, putting your body in that compromised condition basically guarantees that you will overeat to compensate.

She said that one of the easiest ways to gauge your hunger is to rate it on a scale of one to ten. "Do you think you would be able to apply a number to your hunger?" she asked.

I looked at her confidently. "Um, can I? I basically invented scales of one to ten," and then I told her about my Emotional Rating System (it's in the appendix of this book), and I'm pretty sure she was impressed, but she played it cool, because she's a professional. Essentially, on a scale of one to ten, one being fucking starving and ten being way too full, she said you want to be able to recognize when you're in the four to seven range and stay there. Framing hunger in this fashion was really helpful for me, and I think I'd been waiting for someone to tell me, officially, that I should never let myself get to a place where I am starving and ready to cut a bitch.

She also talked about the idea of mindful eating, which is basically slowing down, focusing on the food you're consuming, and staying in the moment. Mindful eating can also include journaling to identify your feelings, so you can figure out if you're eating to numb an emotion, and if so, what the real problem is. She told me that if I'm eyes-deep in a bowl of buttery pasta, I can stay there, but I need to take a minute to ask myself, "Why am I eating this?" That doesn't mean I have to stop eating right away, but it's about identifying your triggers and putting small measures in place to protect yourself. It wasn't groundbreaking, but it was presented in a way that felt healthy and attainable and fundamental—plus I still got to eat the pasta. After trying this a couple of times, taking that pause was enough to give me some perspective, and understanding my triggers became more interesting than finishing the pasta. She also suggested I choose a friend to call when I felt the urge to binge and give myself permission to eat a piece of bread at a restaurant without feeling like I'd screwed up so much that I might as well down the entire basket. It was all about setting some boundaries and forgiving myself when I broke them. After all, half my emotional eating is some form of punishment for other emotional eating, and I know this is very common. It's like, *Fuck you, you ate a Quarter Pounder with cheese yesterday, so tonight you're eating pizza just to get back at yourself.*

In the years since Andrew left and I decided to take control of my eating, my relationship with food has drastically changed, and so has my relationship with my body. What I've learned over that time is that if your motivation is weight loss or a certain size, it never works. I wanted my brain and body to feel better, and that started happening long before I saw any change in the mirror. But then one day I did, and that was a nice surprise. I look good because I feel good.

Today, I'm all about moderation. I know that sounds cliché, but it really is the case. I eat whatever I want, but I want less because my relationship to food has changed, and I'm healthier emotionally. I don't eat a whole pizza, I eat a slice—fine, two slices. And I don't keep things like doughnuts in the house, because I want to set myself up for success, and I know that if something comes into my house I'm going to eat it. That said, I will drive to the store to get a doughnut if I really, really, really need one, and sometimes, quite frankly, I really do need a doughnut. I try to pay attention to when I feel full. I exercise because I enjoy the way I feel afterward, not because I need to check a box. The body I see in the mirror is strong and, more important, if I never saw another mirror again it would be okay, because my body feels like me.

Chapter 12

Better Than Great,
Less Than Perfect

Okay, before we go any further, I should stop and say a few things about the ego, especially as it relates to the topic of self-doubt. That voice in your head? The one saying you're not good enough or that you're worthless or that your ass is too fat? That's your ego.

Think about the last time you were really embroiled in a moment of self-doubt. You could hear the critical voice as if it were sitting on your shoulder and whispering in your ear. Now think about this: if you can hear the voice talking to you, then it can't really be you.

And if it's not your own voice, whose voice is it?

Well, no one's actually. It's a protective mechanism, developed to help keep us from getting eaten by lions or some other horrible fate. In the old days the voice would yell, "Run, run, ruuuuuuuuunnnnnnnn!" and that's what we would do. Today, we've pretty much evolved beyond lion-eating threats, but the ego has endured, instilling fear, doubt, and worry in the name of safety, because the ego doesn't know that circumstances have changed, and it needs a job.

It's easy to get derailed or discouraged by this critical voice, the one delivering that near-constant play-by-play of all the ways in which you are less than and you should be better. I once read that in order to tame it and mini- mize self-doubt, you should treat it as a roommate who lives inside your head in order to put just a tiny bit of distance between you and your thoughts. (The book was *The Untethered Soul* by Michael A. Singer, and it's one of my favorites.) I found this to be really helpful, because it taught me that I can just ask her to be quiet when she's causing more harm than good, which, for example, is what I did when I wanted to tame my anxiety. *Thanks for your help today, but I'm fine. I'm going it alone—don't need your input. Please go back in your room. I'll call you if I need you.*

Imagine if a friend came over and you asked how you looked in an outfit and she said, "Well, I can see cellulite on your legs, and your ankles are kind of thick, and you didn't shave, and you're a little bit fat, and your hair looks weird." You'd probably want to say, "Okay, um, can you leave?" Once I could see the voice in my head in that light, I was able to gain some perspective on the self-doubt I'd carried with me for decades. Maybe I didn't have to be so beholden to everything it said. Maybe I could just ask it to go away.

When I was young, I mistook the voice in my head for my mother's voice—she criticized me a lot, and also, as you know, our voices sound the same. And honestly something she said might have planted an early seed of doubt—none of us are born with negative self-talk on an endless loop—but that seed turned into a plant that was nurtured by me, with a little help from mean girls and perfectly sized models on magazines, and let us not forget social media, that fast-paced filtered version of other people's lives that can be accessed all day, all night, at home, at work, and even in your car. (If you want a quick reminder of just how "less than" you are, just fire up the world wide web. Comparison is the thief of joy.)

Some of us hear that ongoing narrative in our heads

very loud and clear, and I, for better and worse, am one of those people. And while I've gotten better at taming it, that voice of self-doubt still sneaks back in at especially vulnerable moments.

This happened to an extreme degree just last year, when I first launched my podcast. (*Jen Gotch is OK . . . Sometimes*. Available wherever podcasts are . . . sold? Streamed? I don't know, but you should definitely check it out.) It was an entirely new creative endeavor for me, and an especially intimate one at that. With ban.do, my ideas were literally for sale, but with the podcast I was the commodity. It was just me and the microphone, in the listener's ear, for thirtyish minutes a week. Podcasting is an exceedingly personal pursuit, and even just planning for it fanned the self-doubt flames. *Are my ideas any good? Is my voice pleasant to listen to? Why would anyone even care about this?*

Then, before the podcast even launched, I was on the phone with my producer, Serena, talking about advertisers and our long-term plans for the series. Or, at least, we started to talk about those things, but then Serena—lovely, sweet, well-meaning Serena—said one innocent thing that sent me into a spiral of self-doubt. She was running through different scenarios of how to handle advertisers in different situations and she said something like, "Then, if the podcast tanks . . ." She followed this up with a helpful suggestion of something we could do, because of course not everything works and there is always a way to right the ship, but I didn't hear anything after the word "tanks" because "tanks" means you could fail, which means you *will* fail, which means . . . *What the fuck did I think I was doing? How could I possibly think for one second that I could host a podcast? Who would ever want to listen to me?* Suddenly words like "talentless" and "unoriginal" and "humiliating" were having a field day in my mind. I plowed through, because we had episodes to produce, but it wasn't easy. (Imagine, then, how writing an entire book about my life has felt.)

Even when we know we shouldn't listen, the voice in our head tells us we need to be perfect, or that we aren't perfect, or that we aren't enough. But perfection is a myth. If there's anything I know for sure, it's that. And I learned that with a little help from ban.do.

Ban.do has always been an extension of me and a reflection of my personality, and in the early days, in and among the laughter, glitter, and confetti, there was anxiety and self-doubt. I was grinding all the time, because there was always something that could be done to make everything better. I pored over the smallest details, unwilling to send something out into the world that wasn't "perfect." At first, that attitude contributed to our success. Everything could always be more right. And more right. And perhaps we achieved greatness faster than we might have if we didn't care and didn't sweat the small stuff. But then we sold the company, and we had to scale. We had to create more products in greater quantities, and it was no longer an intimate endeavor. I wasn't able to indulge myself over the small details, because doing so would hold up production and hurt the business. It wasn't sustainable. Eventually I had to let go and throw up my hands, which meant things that felt very imperfect—like glaringly not okay, in my opinion—went out into the world. And, as it turned out, they sold just as well. I still remember the pain and agony that came when, after developing one of our first thermal mugs, the sample arrived in our office and THE LID WAS TWO SHADES OFF AND WE WERE ALL GOING TO DIE. A small group of us sat in the office holding Pantone chips up to the mug and crying. Like actually crying tears. I'm sure the guys at Lifeguard Press, who'd been doing this for years, were thinking, *What are you all so fucking worried about?* But I was a highly sensitive person struggling with perfectionism, and I was leading a team of women who were very much the same, and we were all devastated. There was no time for another round of samples—and even if there had been, this could have gone on endlessly—so we had to approve the mug then or not produce it at all. I reluctantly okayed it, and, six months later, the mug was released—and would you believe it if I told you that not only did no one die but also people loved it and it sold incredibly well?

Of course, I wasn't convinced immediately—changing your entire perspective on what is good enough and what isn't takes time and experience. So a different version of that same lesson had to be repeated many, many times, but eventually I got it. It helped that the evidence was right there in the sales data.

Although holding ourselves and our work to impossible standards is unhealthy, aspiring to greatness is certainly a worthy pursuit. My own goal, for work but also for life, is to be better than great but less than perfect. It's my advice to you: bring your A game, do your best, but let that be enough and be able to recognize when it crosses over into being excessive. I think we can all manage that. Perfection is a myth, but that doesn't mean we just give up. It means we have to have perspective and backup from the picture of whatever it is we're scrutinizing in order to get a better view. From that vantage point, you'll probably notice that you're doing pretty great, and you might have set the bar too high.

The other day I was sitting on the toilet, where all great thinking happens, and I had an epiphany. I was staring at a shirt I'd left on the floor—a vintage, white, high-collared, button-up-the-back, lace-trimmed shirt (if you know me or even follow me on Instagram, you know this style of blouse is an addiction of mine), that I bought a few weeks earlier at the Rose Bowl flea market. It's probably the twentieth shirt in this same style I've bought there this year, but it was incredibly soft and, like, eight bucks, so I pulled the trigger. When I got home, I realized it was missing three of the six back buttons. I never scrutinize clothes when I buy them, since impulse buying is way more fun than scrutiny, especially when the clothes are eight dollars, so I couldn't be all that mad about it. I love this shirt. I've worn it with pride many times in the few weeks I've had it. Too many times, probably, but I'm nothing if not loyal. The first few times I wore it I just said, "Fuck it," and went on with my day with the back of my shirt half unbuttoned. Eventually that seemed ridiculous, so I found some small gold safety pins and used them as substitute buttons. But as I sat there peeing, gazing upon this blouse, it occurred to me that maybe I should take the next step and have some buttons put on. *Maybe I'll take it to the seamstress down the street,* I thought. *She probably has some buttons sitting around that might come close to matching the existing ones. Or maybe she'll suggest we switch out all the buttons so that it looks better.* But that notion kind of offended me, on behalf of the shirt. "No!" I said firmly to myself. I said it out loud because, well, I'm alone a lot so it's okay to talk to yourself while you're staring at a blouse and peeing. I would actually prefer the buttons to be mismatched, I realized, even though that meant the shirt would be imperfect. I liked the blouse I bought, and its imperfections show that it's had a life. I don't know where it's been, but I bet it's been an adventure. The realization prompted me to survey all the possessions in my line of sight, and it was clear—chipped glasses, worn-in shoes, paint-stained overalls—I don't shy away from imperfection. And it doesn't just apply to material goods. I'm intrigued by visual "flaws" in other people too. They're just so much more interesting. Sitting there, still peeing, it hit me: I've always accepted imperfection, in everything and everyone but myself and my creations.

My goals for the future are to accept my own imperfections just as I accept the flaws of my favorite shirt. If I wait until I feel perfect in order to be happy with myself, I will be spinning my wheels forever. Self-acceptance is the antidote to self-doubt, and it's kryptonite for perfection.

I'm getting better at this, but I'm a work in progress. I have learned, for example, to accept the aging process. When I look at my face in the mirror I just think, *this is what forty-seven is supposed to look like, and it'll be interesting to see what happens as I get older*. But, at the same time, I'm hard on myself when it comes to my body. Everyone's hang-ups are different, so you might be thinking, *My work has to be perfect*, or *My cabinets have to look perfect*. But if you realize that those are self-perpetuating ideas, it can be really liberating. When I catch myself slipping into the destructive self-talk spiral, I can identify what's happening, and that the voice is just my ego. I can acknowledge that there is zero benefit to looking in the mirror and listening to that voice admonish me. *You're a fat, ugly asshole*, it says, but I'm not interested in hearing that. As a result, I feel a lot better about myself than I once did.

When I do find myself succumbing to self-doubt and perfectionism, I try to ask myself one question: *Did I do my best?* If I know the answer is yes, then I feel good. There's no more reason to doubt myself. (I once made myself a sweatshirt with iron-on letters that read "I DID MY BEST," and men and women of all ages would stop me on the street to ask where I got it. We ended up creating the shirt for ban.do and putting the phrase on a variety of products, and they were all huge sellers. The point is, I'm obviously not the only one who benefits from this reminder.)

We live in a world that increasingly embraces the unre-touched and unfiltered. There's a reason for that, and it's a helpful reminder for all of us. What's perfect is so much less interesting than what's real.

Chapter 13

What Does Your Necklace Say?

For nearly a decade, ban.do was my baby. Creating and maintaining the company felt like my life's purpose, but ten years in, debating Pantone colors and coffee phrases— *Not without my coffee* or *More coffee, please?*—started to feel meaningless. I was growing and evolving, and I wanted my growth reflected in the brand.

But how the fuck was I going to do that?

The answer came to me toward the end of December 2017, a couple of days before Christmas. I was sitting in my pj's at my dining room table, sipping on my Bulletproof coffee, when I was struck by lightning. Okay, fine, I wasn't, but that's what it felt like. It was that sudden. I wasn't thinking about anything other than how good butter in coffee really is and then the next thing I knew there was a fully formed thought in my head. It was pure intuition, or even a spirit. I know that sounds like a ghost got into my head, but as someone who has to ideate all the time, there's a completely different feeling to an intuitive idea from one you brainstormed. With the former, you just know in your gut you've tapped into something good and pure.

I envisioned two necklaces, one that read "Anxiety" and another that read "Depression." The idea was to inspire conversation around these issues by making something very small and personal and intentional for the person wearing it. It wouldn't be something that someone could spot across the room, but the person standing next to you might ask, "What does your necklace say?" And you'd tell them, and they might say, "I have anxiety too," or "Do you have bad anxiety?" or just "Oh," and walk away, but we didn't need to talk to them anyway. Having words like "anxiety" and "depression" out in the open normalizes them and reduces stigma, and for the people wearing them, the necklaces would serve as a way to own or accept their mental health struggles.

Keep in mind that, at least as I see it, I'd been a mental

health advocate for long before these necklaces occurred to me. It's just that, for most of those years, my advocacy had a smaller reach—basically just my family, friends, and coworkers, an occasional waiter, and this one lady in an elevator. My more public mental health advocacy began during my trial separation with Andrew. He was in Australia and I was living alone at home in LA for the first time in forever, so I decided to dip my toes into Snapchat. Mostly because I needed someone to talk to at night, and a bunch of strangers in my phone made the most sense. I was already on Instagram, but Stories weren't a thing yet and Snapchat felt more intimate, so I started filming myself talking, first just about basic stuff like how my day went, then eventually revealing if I was feeling anxious, or sad, or in desperate need of a Tate's chocolate chip cookie—and then, of course, filming myself eating a whole bag. At one point I basically had a talk show where I interviewed my dog, Phil, and chased around my cat, Gertie, asking if she wanted a hug (she didn't). It seems everyone really enjoyed seeing a C-level executive be accessible and generally quite wacky, because my followers grew quickly. This was before influencers were really letting their guard down and getting personal on social media, and I was unknowingly putting myself out there in a pretty vulnerable way, just by being me. I started carrying some of that over to my Instagram feed, replacing brunch photos with longer posts about feelings that no one really seemed to be talking about. People would message me to say how brave they thought I was to be sharing these experiences. And yet for me it wasn't scary at all. I didn't really give it a second thought. Sure, I knew on some level that I was taking a risk—both personal and professional—by talking about some really personal stuff, especially surrounding mental illness, but each time I published one of those posts, I'd feel a little ping in my gut. By then, I was familiar enough with that feeling to know it was a sign I was onto something.

It became clear pretty quickly that my candor and honesty were having a positive impact on people. It started with those messages from followers, which also said things like "How did you know how I'm feeling???" or "Thank you for bringing attention to this!" And eventually evolved into people stopping me on the street, asking me if I was Jen Gotch, and then giving me a very long, hard hug. I was in heaven, because the posts married two of my favorite things: *I can express my every emotion publicly* AND *help people?* It was my dream. Hearing that my suffering wasn't singular, although kind of heartbreaking, was also really reassuring. It's always nice to know that, as humans, we're all struggling with a lot of the same issues. Plenty of people are embarrassed or scared to reveal so much of themselves so publicly, which is quite reasonable, but somehow I missed that humility gene, or just the concept of personal boundaries. I don't know exactly why I've never had any fear around exposing my thoughts and feelings in such a raw way. It must have been all those years in talk therapy—you just get used to sharing. I can't remember the last time I simply said "Good," when someone asked me how I was doing. If you are going to inquire, expect a very honest answer. With details. Lots and lots of details.

Eventually I left the intimacy of Snapchat and succumbed to the power of Instagram Stories, where my reach was much larger. I continued giving an unfiltered look at my mental health struggles, rating my moods, having anxiety attacks at airports, and inadvertently torturing my cat with my attempts at affection. The support and gratitude continued to pour in. After all, forty million adults in the United States are affected by anxiety disorders. In 2018 nearly one in twelve adults reported feeling depressed. Which means that most everyone who was watching my Stories either struggled with these mental health issues or knew someone who did, and in talking about it, I was helping to remove the stigma. Without intending to, I was slowly becoming a mental health advocate, and although I was slightly reluctant to accept that title, on many levels it felt good.

In late 2017 my friend Sophia Amoruso, founder and CEO of Girlboss, asked me to host a mental health podcast on her network. At first I said yes to the podcast and no to the mental health part, because I still couldn't really wrap my head around this advocate idea, but isn't it funny and strange how often other people see our strengths and purpose before we do? Eventually I came around to the podcast, and in the process of concepting it, I slowly, but eagerly, started to embrace my new advocate identity.

As my personal passion for opening up conversations around mental health continued to grow, my perspective on ban.do—and my goals for its evolution—started to shift. Here was this big company, with a much larger reach than I had, but I couldn't find a point of entry (OMG, fine, that's what she said) to continue these conversations with our customers and community. Talking about mental health around the office was one thing, but speaking to our customers about it was another. Ban.do is a pretty mainstream company, and at that point in time, we were known as the "fun" brand. Not because that was how I planned it or even wanted it, but because that was the word people used to describe us. Conventional wisdom at the time was that the biggest thing a brand could hope for was to be known for something specific, so to be the "fun brand" was actually a big win no matter how trivialized it made me feel.

But when the necklace idea hit me, the force of it convinced me I had to pursue it. Like right away. I had an acquaintance, Ivka, who owned a jewelry design company, so I emailed her that night and we set up a meeting for right after the New Year. The energy around this idea was moving so fast that at first I seriously wondered if I should just set up an Etsy shop, which was ridiculous considering I already led the creative side of a company with a large base of loyal customers. But jewelry that touched on something as personal as mental illness felt like too big a departure for ban.do, which had never veered into territory that could even remotely be considered touchy or controversial. We decided early on that we wanted to bring positivity to people's lives without veering into areas like politics. But the more I thought about it, the more I realized the necklaces I was picturing could be a natural fit for the company. Everything we had ever created, as far back as when I was working with Jamie, had been about connecting with people, making them feel good, and encouraging joy. And we'd been using words and phrases to resonate with customers for ages, so the necklaces seemed like a departure, maybe, but a logical and natural next step.

I knew that I would need to convince our CEO, David, that the necklaces were a good idea, and honestly, doing so was easier than I thought. After years of working together, building the business and quoting *Seinfeld*, we had become very close and built a lot of trust. He taught me about patience, spreadsheets, and leadership, and I taught him about triggers, bipolar disorder, and anxiety. We have developed a real partnership, and the fact that he let me move forward with this idea was a real show of faith in me. In the end, the necklaces became a meaningful collaboration for us.

By March 2018 the necklaces were on sale. But only for a few hours, because that's how long it took the first batch to sell out. They sold out faster than anything ban.do had sold in years. I was at a speaking engagement in Washington, DC, on the day the necklaces launched, and when I finished speaking, I had a slew of excited and congratulatory text messages from friends and coworkers and my dad, and one from David that just read, "Something's happening."

I wasn't especially shocked, but I was definitely excited.

When an idea is good enough, you just know. But then, almost as quickly as the necklaces sold out, the backlash on our Instagram account began. I had become accustomed to opening up about my own mental illness on social media, and I'd only ever gotten positive feedback, so I didn't see this coming. But there seemed to be a fifty-fifty split between those who applauded our efforts to destigmatize mental illness and those who were angry that a company would glamorize mental health struggles and make them fashionable. They left angry comments and sent angry emails—I even received a death threat, which just goes to show how triggering this topic can be. Some people were also mad that we would exploit mental illness for profit—which, of course, we weren't, because we teamed up with the mental health awareness nonprofit Bring Change to Mind, and 100 percent of the net proceeds went to them.

I was really frustrated that so many people misunderstood our intention, because I had taken for granted that everyone who knows ban.do knows me (which, if you look at the numbers, is clearly not possible), and no one on my Instagram had ever questioned my motives or my message. But when we called the folks at Bring Change to Mind to ask what we should do, they made it clear that as long as we were active in the mental health space, we were going to have detractors. Anxiety and depression are touchy subjects, with a lot of associated (and unnecessary) shame. Plenty of people don't want to discuss them publicly.

Still, I took the negative feedback seriously. I had some really healthy conversations with a few of the naysayers who messaged me because I wanted to understand their viewpoint, and when I went back and did a gut check, I still felt like we hadn't done anything wrong. I understood why the necklaces were upsetting for some people, but we were promoting them for all the right reasons.

There was a whole other camp of people—all those customers who snatched up necklaces in that first release—who loved what we were doing. Not only were they supporting the necklaces, but they wanted other variations to represent their other issues. Requests came in for options like "OCD" or "ADD" and even "endometriosis." Ultimately we decided to stick to the words that were related to my own experience. Words that I could, and already did, speak to personally. That way we could show there was a real person behind the cause.

The mixed reaction was a reminder of how far we've come in regard to mental health, how far we still have to go, and also how triggering the issues can be. As happy as I was to see how many people were buying necklaces, it was also disheartening. The anxiety necklace sells more than any of the others, and frankly it makes me sad that so many people identify with it, but it also fuels my desire to help. I know what anxiety feels like, and I know it doesn't feel good. And I know that most people don't have the luxury of spending as much time and money as I have trying to wriggle out of it.

As I watched the momentum behind the jewelry build, I knew we had hit a turning point for ban.do. "We popped the bubble," I kept saying in every meeting. I'm not even sure I knew what that meant, but I knew for sure that the pivot and growth I was craving for ban.do was now possible, and I was thrilled. Not just for me but also for all of us who work at the company and share my passion for evoking joy in people and connecting with them on a meaningful level. Moving forward we'd be able to dig into more grown-up conversations, instead of always being like, "Have fun today, have fun every day!" I mean, that's a great sentiment, but it can get repetitive. The necklace initiative positioned both me and the company as champions of mental health, which has been incredibly fulfilling. I continue to candidly share about my trials and triumphs on my personal platforms, and ban.do has established an entire focus on helping our customers feel better, through raising money (more than $120,000 to date) and awareness.

When you start a company, it's hard to think about much other than staying afloat, but over time it becomes increasingly important to align the business with your values if you plan to stay on long-term. Now that ban.do has come to represent a cause, I've noticed a difference in our employees too. People are happy to work at a company that stands for something. And I am excited to continue to add meaning to this endeavor, for them and for me.

I know I'm not going to change the world overnight with a collection of jewelry. But the necklaces—which eventually expanded to include the words "resilience" and "bipolar" and the number "7.8" (which, for me, is "just right" on the Emotional Rating System's scale of one to ten)—were pivotal for me because they established me as a mental health advocate. And I finally accepted that role, which will no doubt change the course of my life, and hopefully the life of ban.do too.

Chapter 14

Jen Gotch Wants You to Feel Better (Just Like She Does!)

Giving advice is my default—just ask anyone who has ever worked with me or shared a meal with me or ridden an elevator with me—because I truly believe my life's purpose is to use the learnings from my own life to help others grow and find relief. When we were designing the packaging for the mental health awareness necklaces at ban.do, I insisted that the boxes read, "Jen Gotch wants you to feel better." And that is the fucking truth.

The first time I was asked to write a book—long before I had any business writing a book—I replied with an immediate YES! I had an idea of what the book would be: cover-to-cover advice from me. Anything from how to handle a breakup to how to hire your first employee to how to open a pickle jar. The publisher didn't go for it—too confusing where to shelve it in the bookstore—so I'll tell you here.

Be kind, honest, and stick to your guns.

Find someone who is passionate about your business and can do the things that you shouldn't be doing at a price you can afford.

Either wedge a (dull) knife in between the top of the jar and lid until you hear the vacuum seal break, or put a large rubber band around the lid and twist.

OMG, I can't believe I actually got to put that in a book. Flash-forward five years to a time that made sense for me to write a book. I prepared to put together all my self-help content, but two very wise people (my agent and my editor, if we're naming names—hey, Monika; hey, Lauren) convinced me that sharing my story alongside the advice would be more resonant, and I hope at this point in the book, you feel like they were right. That said, I was able to negotiate one chapter of blatant self-help and holistic betterment, so here we are.

You might be wondering why Jen Gotch—work-crier,

semi-reluctant mental health advocate, and founder of a joyful lifestyle brand—gets to offer up this advice. Well, because after a lifetime of trying to find my equilibrium— on the wrong medications, then the right ones, then off and back on again; single then married then single again; busy, really busy, so fucking busy, not that busy; fluctuating weight and zigzagging career and feeling anxious and then not—I finally feel good. It's like I've made my way back home to myself, and I want to share the insight I've gained along the way.

To me, one of the most vital parts of self-help is self-care. There's a difference: Self-help is the long-term pursuit of feeling better; self-care is made up of the short-term strategies that help you on that journey. You don't need me to tell you that self-care has become a huge trend these days, but it's something I've subscribed to (and ban.do has encouraged) since long before it was a buzzword. I'm thrilled that people are increasingly focused on how to take care of themselves, but I also think it's a sign that, collectively, we aren't feeling all that great. There are any number of reasons for this, from our insistence on being busy at all times, to the constant judgment and comparison that comes from social media, to the state of planet Earth. (Remember when the fear of climate change gave Amabella an anxiety attack on *Big Little Lies*? That shit is real.)

When you go to the doctor, the first question they ask is "What's wrong?" What's hurting? The same question pertains to self-care. Are you down because you've been eating like shit for six months and now you feel shame? Or is it that the useless voice in your head has been repeatedly telling you you're worthless? The possible remedies for "I'm stressed out" are different from those for "I can't seem to get out of bed and I'm completely unmotivated to talk to other people." Eating like shit for six months may seem pretty bad, but the real question is *why* have you been doing that? Because you're trying to numb feelings of loss? Or avoid a hard conversation? So, step one: ask yourself, *What is the problem? How does it make me feel? And is there an underlying layer that's at the root of my suffering? What is the why beneath the why, beneath the why?*

A word of warning: healing comes slower when you're dealing with root causes, which is what I'm suggesting here. Really feeling better is a long-term pursuit and an exercise in patience. Self-care, used correctly, is there to help you on your journey. It is one part of a larger solution. Think of self-help as tending your lawn. Mowing the grass is a quick fix—you cut it off at the surface, and things look better in the short-term—but the grass and the weeds always grow back. But when you're really focused on weeding, you've got to dig deep. I used to sit on my hands and knees in the backyard for hours, meticulously digging up weeds with a small shovel to make sure I got all the roots. That's the kind of emotional excavation necessary to ensure you won't be dealing with the same issue again next week.

One of the first and most important acts of self-care is being honest about what actually makes you feel better. This is harder than it seems at a time when self-care has come to include everything from a face mask to a Netflix binge to buying yourself a new purse. Treating yourself to a doughnut might really be self-care, but numbing yourself with an entire box? That's just avoidance. A great massage will reduce stress, but it doesn't treat anxiety, and at this point we know a candlelit manicure not only gives you flame fingers, but it also does not treat depression. Alleviating symptoms has value (relief, not numbing, is a necessary part of self-care), but if you're looking for a long-term solution you need to be willing to do some hard work. It's like having a deep wound on your arm and putting a Band-Aid on a Band-Aid on a Band-Aid on a Band-Aid in order to help it heal. Suddenly you're wearing seventeen Band-Aids and you have no idea if the wound is better and it gets increasingly difficult to wear long-sleeved shirts.

Sometimes a Band-Aid is all you need, but other times a cut needs stitches, or on rare occasions, surgery.

Because I have decades of experience under my belt, I can usually tell if, for example, I'm staying in bed all day because I truly need a day off, or if it's because I'm overwhelmed and feeling avoidant and I would actually be better off if I tackled an item on my to-do list. But tuning into those needs is a skill that takes practice.

The next step is to identify any adjustments you can make in the short-term. Maybe you need more, or less, or better sleep. Maybe you need to improve your diet, or cut out stress. For me, self-care is a daily practice. I take my meds. I go to my doctors annually, even the dentist, which is really saying something, because for a decade I feared dentists almost as much as I once feared planes. I go to bed and wake up at the same time each day, which has a really positive effect on me, as does making the bed. It's such an easy way to start the day with a win, and to send yourself the message, first thing, that you deserve to be treated well and that you believe in treating yourself well. I just started doing this recently, and the return on investment has been surprisingly huge. I also have that Wednesday night standing date with fun. You will never feel your best if you don't have any pure enjoyment in your life.

Ultimately what I am encouraging is holistic betterment—I consider my physical and mental health, and my emotional and professional well-being, so that I'm caring for my full self and no single aspect of my life dominates the others. (Or, alternatively, so that no one area falls apart while I'm focused elsewhere.)

Depending on what's going on in my life, my self-help and self-care needs change. I'm excited to share what has worked for me, but let me say up front that I know the depth and breadth of some of these strategies might be overwhelming, so don't be intimidated. Take from this list whatever suits you now, and pick whichever strategy sounds the most doable. Start there. And if you're feeling good right now? YAY. But it might be helpful to dog-ear this page should you find yourself slipping into a bad habit or in need of a little care. Remember, you have your whole life. The fact that you bought and are reading this book is already a huge step in the right direction.

So, like I said, my needs often depend on the day or

situation. If I'm dealing with a lot of anxiety, I might need to cut out caffeine or focus on mindfulness or simply pay better attention to my breathing. If I can tell I'm in the midst of a hypomanic episode, it might mean making an appointment with a therapist. If I'm feeling overworked, I may need to be stricter about drawing boundaries around my personal time.

Some self-care strategies are beneficial no matter the root of your struggles. I'm a huge believer in journaling, or documenting your feelings in whatever way works for you—it doesn't have to be a whole "dear diary" thing, it can be as simple as rating your emotions each day. (For inspiration, take a look at my Emotional Rating System at the end of this book.) This is a big part of what I do to understand my own emotional cycles, because on paper I can see, *Hey, wow, I had eight really bad days this month. That seems like too many.* Sometimes the simple act of identifying and labeling your mood is the first step to improving it.

I'd also suggest looking at your relationships—with friends, colleagues, partners—and asking yourself, *Do they lift me up? Do they encourage good behaviors or bad? How am I operating in the relationship? Am I my best self?* The answers might not thrill you, and you might not want to deal with it just yet, and that's okay. Take your time. Patience. When I made the commitment to really feeling better, I had to cut out some toxic relationships, and it was hard and painful because they were relationships with people I loved, but in the end, everyone involved is better for it.

In the course of my healing, I've also gone to acupuncture and used healing crystals and now I see a Reiki healer. I live in LA, after all, where alternative healing is mainstream and mainstream healing is, well, kind of alternative. Bettie, my Reiki healer, has become a force in my life and my spiritual teacher. She's also the person who manages my expectations when I want to declare myself cured or, even, enlightened.

"I want to get there," I'll say. "Am I there?"

"That's not how it works," she reminds me. "It's the journey."

Today, I feel good. This is partly due to the self-care I've talked about here, but it's in large part due to all the other work I've done, including fighting for the right diagnosis and logging hours in therapy, and getting a handle on my ego. My mental illnesses have stabilized.

They're still a part of me, but certainly not the major factor that they once were, which, if you're struggling with mental illness right now, I hope you find reassuring. That doesn't mean I won't have another flare-up—I could wake up tomorrow with a depressive episode. I don't think I will, because I've worked really hard to set myself up for success, but it could absolutely happen. And if it doesn't happen tomorrow, it will certainly happen eventually. But I don't measure my healing by whether I have another episode, I measure it by how I handle those episodes when they hit. My goal is not to ignore the feelings or to conquer them, it's simply to not let them swallow me whole.

I could not possibly point to any one thing as *the* factor that "healed" me. I wish it were that simple, but nothing this good comes easy. I got here by being pushed into really uncomfortable places and then pushing myself into more uncomfortable places. By hitting rock bottom and then finding a place below rock bottom. By actively facing my fears. By admitting defeat and asking for help and then accepting help too. By ending relationships that weren't serving me, no matter the guilt and pain associated with those decisions, and by trusting my gut and intuition—that soft whisper that resides in all of us.

It's an invisible magic that is hard to believe in, but once you do, damn if it doesn't make life a lot less painful and complex.

None of this means I don't sometimes get too drunk or sleep in or skip working out for two weeks straight. It just means that when I do, I keep moving rather than shaming myself for the lapse. As far as I can tell, that's the biggest win of all. I've created a new normal that I can actually sustain.

During a recent visit to Florida to see my parents, I decided to take a ride on an electric skateboard. This might not seem like a big deal, but for someone who has lived in fear of doing anything that could possibly end in injury, it was pretty major. Six months before writing this book, there's not a chance I would have stepped on that floating death trap. And it ended as I could have predicted: with me on the ground, my arm severely scraped up, and my tailbone throbbing. For days it hurt to walk, and a scab emerged over a third of my forearm. I was so proud. I was scared and I got hurt and I survived.

A couple of days later, I was on a walk with my brother. He looked at me with an expression that was part confusion and part skepticism. "You've changed a lot," he said. "You seem better."

I'm proud of the fact that I feel good, and proud that the people in my life can see my evolution. I believe I am worthy of feeling good. I believe we all are. And it doesn't scare me to know that feelings are temporary. I have found a way to enjoy both feeling good and feeling bad, and I hope that this book (and the next one, wink wink) will help get you there too, because it is a fucking fantastic way to feel.

Chapter 15

The Upside of Being Down

In just a few pages, you'll see my author bio. "Jen Gotch is genetically predisposed to optimism." I can't prove it's actually in my genes (my bloodline has seen some bad shit, but they've also survived it), but it sure feels like optimism is hard-coded in there somewhere. I use that line whenever I'm asked to describe myself, because after this whole journey, the fact that I continue to see the upside in any situation is what makes me, me.

Optimism is crucial to who I am. It's honestly one of the most important principles of my life and has gotten me to where I am today. Optimism has informed my personality, my brand, my relationships, my approach to mental health and mental illness, and sometimes simply my ability to get out of bed in the morning. I'm certain it can serve the same purpose for you. I'm not talking about a well-intentioned but ultimately hollow "look on the bright side!" when things have gone horribly wrong, because even when the person who says that means well, it's totally normal and acceptable to want to punch them in their smiling face. I'm talking about the ability to see the way out—or at least believe there *will* be a way out—of difficult times. To know at a cellular level that things will be okay. That sort of optimism is critical to resilience, and you don't fight your way through decades of struggles with mental illness and come out on top without a boatload of resilience.

Developing an optimistic outlook, especially if you're someone who defaults to pessimism, is almost an act of mind control. Negative thinking is totally normal, we all do it, but it's incredibly limiting. And if you struggle with anxiety, negative thinking can almost become a way of life. I once read that we have over fifty thousand thoughts each day, and an estimated 70 to 80 percent of those thoughts are negative. But I promise you, reframing that mind-set is worth it. You may not always be able to prevent negative thoughts from popping up, but you can certainly recognize them, keep them in perspective, and work to control your reaction to them. You can approach your thoughts with gratitude and patience instead of fear. It makes the hard times just a tad easier, and the good times more fun. It will make you the kind of person others want to be around, and more important, it will make you the kind of person *you* want to be around.

Honing your ability to see the upside of being down is one of the kindest and most valuable things you can do for yourself. It's a process, and it can't necessarily happen overnight, but, for me, the decision to switch from pessimism to optimism actually did.

It was my sophomore year of college, and I was living with two girls, Carrie and Beth, who I had become friends with when we were freshmen. Beth and Carrie were debutantes from an upper-class parochial high school, and they carried themselves how I imagined all rich people did. I had seen that kind of poise and confidence in the movies and on *Dynasty*, but never in real life. While my family was definitely upper-middle class, we weren't filthy rich, and the difference seemed to be that Beth and Carrie had a baked-in confidence that came from having everything they ever wanted. They each drove a Mercedes and had

Louis Vuitton purses and I didn't know I needed either one of those things until I saw them close-up.

When we were freshmen, Beth and Carrie lived across the hall from me. I was intrigued, so I watched them from afar during the first few weeks of school—well, from across the hall if we are being literal, and through the peephole of my dorm room if we are being really literal. I decided, after a handful of casual hellos in the dorm hallway, that I would make a grand gesture in order to win their friendship, so I went across the hall and offered them my last two Twizzlers. They accepted, and our relationship took off from there. We took road trips to the beach and convinced strangers to buy us beer from 7-Eleven. We walked to campus trading stories about how awful our professors were and sat in our dorm eating Little Caesars pizza and watching *Oprah*. We watched a lot of *Oprah*.

For a long time, being friends with Beth and Carrie made me feel legitimate in a way that I hadn't felt before. When I was with them, I felt superior to everyone else, and although it didn't feel completely natural, it did feel strangely powerful. But the thing about Beth and Carrie was that, although poised and wealthy with great clothes and great cars, they weren't especially kind people. In fact, they were basically mean girls, though that wasn't really an expression in the early nineties. They judged everyone around them, subtly being condescending to them and privately disparaging them and just generally complaining and talking about how everyone and everything was the worst. I began to look down on people too, because that's what they did, and when you're nineteen and you decide that someone else knows what's cool, you do what they do.

To be honest, I was pretty good at the whole rude-and-judgy thing. I'm a detail-oriented person and can rip anyone to shreds in thirteen seconds flat without even thinking about it. It made me feel cool and powerful and superior, even if it also felt exhausting and shameful and gross. What I've come to understand over the years is that these judgmental behaviors and negative attitudes are often an attempt to deflect attention from our own pain and insecurity, or to avoid acknowledging them altogether. It's a lot easier to focus on other people's shortcomings than our own.

I didn't entirely understand that when I was nineteen, of course, but I must have had a sense of it deep down, because sometime toward the end of my freshman year I started to think that maybe these were not the right girlfriends for me. It was just a small tug in the back of my mind, and I was still mostly enjoying all the fun and pizza and *Oprah*, so I committed to moving into an apartment with them sophomore year. Still, I was craving other friendships too, and when you're at a huge state school with what feels like three thousand people in your algebra class, you have to make an effort. So I did something I said I never would and joined a sorority. I'd avoided sororities when I was a freshman, because the idea of being surrounded by a large group of bouncy, giggling girls sounded like a nightmare, but after being clouded in negativity for the past year, a house full of good attitudes didn't sound so bad. This new group of girls, many of whom would become lifelong friends, were cheerful and bright and encouraging. They didn't look down on people for sport. Sure there was a little judgment—we were nineteen, after all—but more than that there was acceptance. And that group mind-set resonated with me. It felt right.

Beth and Carrie didn't rush a sorority, probably because they felt like they were above it. So while I was busy with pledging—which entailed having a different activity every night and a pledge class of fifty new friends—our relationship began to strain. I'm sure they thought I had abandoned them.

I don't know what time it was when Beth burst into my room sophomore year, with Carrie on her tail, I just know it was dark out and that I was sound asleep, tucked under my Laura Ashley floral comforter and surrounded by white wicker furniture. Now, listen. I do not like being roused from a deep sleep at all, especially to be yelled at. My mom would do this from time to time. Whatever had made her upset was so energizing that she couldn't wait, she needed answers and she needed them now. It's a crime of passion. But it's disorienting and rude and shocking, especially since sleep is one of my favorite things.

Beth was screaming. "You are the fucking worst friend! Didn't your mom ever teach you how to be a friend?" Maybe she was drunk, I don't know, but she really laid into me, seemingly out of nowhere. To them it probably wasn't out of nowhere. I'm sure they had been discussing what a shithead I was for weeks, and I did share some blame, but my memory is just of pure rage standing over my bed, screaming at me. It was intense and unexpected, and I felt ambushed and scared and sad and mad, but it was also something of an aha moment. The universe was trying to wake me up. What stands out about this incident all these years later, the reason it pops into my head whenever I'm thinking about optimism, is that I remember thinking, as I sat on the receiving end of a verbal thrashing, *I don't want to be like these girls.* For so long I assumed that these were my friends and I should be like them, but suddenly the truth I long believed deep down hit me smack in the face: *These are bad people, and I don't want to live like them. I want to be positive.* I'm sure they weren't actually bad people, but they were certainly negative, and were probably suffering and unhappy, and I'm not sure I knew the difference at the time. I made the decision right then and there that I would no longer focus on how horrible everyone and everything was. I would see the good and approach things with hope, though that shift was not nearly as easy as I thought it would be.

The first step was acknowledging that I wanted to change and then asking myself why I was initially drawn to pessimism—it had a lot to do with feeling cool and superior, as I've already mentioned. I challenged myself to find the upside to every situation, every person, every shitty thing that happened to me (this is the hard part). It was something I practiced for a long time, and only in the last ten years or so have I really been able to embody this attitude and truly understand that there is no good without bad and no bad without good. The bad is there so we can know what good is, but also to teach us something— sometimes something big, sometimes small. But if you can accept the situation rather than resist it, and have gratitude for the potential enlightenment it could bring, you can find peace. With practice, this becomes second nature—and only one person has threatened to punch me in the face.

It took me years before I got really good at embracing positivity. The work is never done. I still pass judgment, but I'm aware of it when it's happening and I do my best to pivot to compassion, and that suits me much better. The memory of that late-night teardown has attached itself to the idea of optimism for me because when you are lying in bed with two nineteen-year-old girls standing over you and screaming, it's pretty memorable, and if their yelling and general negative energy is what prompts you to adopt an entirely new approach to life, well, that's not something you forget.

I'm told by people much wiser and more enlightened than I that my predisposition to optimism is actually not that unique, that optimism is in fact everyone's natural state, but it's easy to get off course, as I did with Beth and Carrie.

When I advocate for optimism, I'm not talking about sugarcoating or putting a positive spin on everything.

I'm talking about acknowledging when things are bad, accepting that, and moving forward with a hopeful outlook rather than a downward spiral.

This mind-set can be applied to every aspect of your life, and if you happen to be in business, especially as a founder or business owner, it will be very useful. When you care that much about what you're doing, it's hard not to worry on an hourly basis, which can easily incite anxiety, and that can act as something of an inhibitor to optimism. (That said, the two *can* coexist. Please don't think that if you struggle with anxiety, you are doomed to a life of pessimism. Seemingly irrational thoughts, like my cat getting killed, are caused by anxiety, which can be a by-product of a very talkative ego. Pessimism is focusing on the negatives in actual, real-life situations.) For many many years at ban.do I was plagued with worry, and it was exhausting and counterproductive. In the company's early days, even the smallest thing, like a single complaint from a customer, made me think the sky was falling. I remember when Todd, one of the owners of both Lifeguard Press and ban.do and a mentor for me in the "not freaking out" department, told me not to worry about it. "One complaint isn't much," he said. "Let me know when there are a thousand." I don't think we've ever hit a thousand, but in the instances when higher-than-average complaints do roll in, he takes it in stride. Todd never seems worried, and if he feels a tinge of it deep down, he certainly doesn't let it dictate his decisions or influence his behavior. At the beginning, I would watch Todd like I was watching a rare bird, and eventually I came to imitate his behavior. I know you're imagining me flapping around the office like a bird, and that's okay.

The most important thing to understand about optimism is that you are in control. You can choose your perspective. There is so much happening around us that we can't control, and even more where we might try our best and things still turn out badly, and there's nothing we can do about it. You can't control the situation, but you can decide how you react to it. Once you get a handle on that, it's a really powerful thing.

Choosing optimism isn't always easy, just as it's not easy to confront the voice in your head when you're facing down an anxiety attack. It takes practice, even when you're faced with situations that are more of a nuisance than a true challenge. Recently I was working from home and I could tell before the day was even half over that it was going to be one of those days where every email, every phone call was one more "You didn't get this" or

"This fell through" or "This isn't working." And it was shitty and I was agitated, but I was able to practice saying, "This is a pain and inconvenient, but it's not a tragedy. I'm going to be okay." It's a good exercise. The next time something bad, or even just annoying, happens, try to take an optimistic approach and see how it feels. If you ask me, it feels like freedom.

Despite everything that happened with Beth and Carrie, I didn't think about optimism so explicitly until I started a company that became known for it. People often tell me they love the phrases on ban.do products because they're so optimistic, and I remember one day thinking, *I came up with a lot of those phrases, so that must be my perspective on life.* I knew I tried to be generally positive—I made that decision in college, after all—but I don't know that I had labeled it as optimism. But ban.do empowered me to claim optimism as my own. Starting a company is interesting in that way—it teaches you a lot about yourself. It strikes me as a little bit like parenting (though I have no experience in parenting, so I might be wrong), because you literally have an external reflection of your ideals and your preferences, so you have no choice but to confront who you are, for better and worse.

This was especially clear with one of our early T-shirts,

which had the phrase "No Bad Days" emblazoned on the front. The phrase, like so many others we use in our product line ("Everything Is Gonna Be Ok," "Pink Skies Up Ahead"), reflects our optimistic outlook and ideally encourages others to adopt it too. What was interesting for me about the No Bad Days shirt was that for what I considered to be a pretty innocuous top, it definitely raised questions for some of my followers on Instagram. Was no bad days really an attainable ideal? And how could I, of all people, advocate for such an unrealistic goal? After all, I'd suffered so many mental health issues and publicly shared many, many bad days. Their questions made me stop and think. How *could* I do that? Was I really suggesting that the goal is to have no bad days? I replied to the people questioning my motives by saying it was meant to be aspirational, but what, exactly, was I asking people to aspire to?

There's no way to avoid days in which bad things happen, but we can control how we label that day. And finding a way to see even the hardest days as okay days, *that* was—and continues to be—the goal.

Today I'm full of hope and optimism and the certainty that everything will work out in the end. To be blissfully aware of your challenges and how you might overcome them, rather than just reflexively finding a bright side without context, that is true optimism. It's a positive, problem-solving attitude that requires trust. Optimists don't obsess over negative circumstances or experiences, but instead they approach them with gratitude, humor, and acceptance. It's not about pretending to be okay, it's about truly believing that everything will be okay eventually, and that you will have a hand in that outcome. This mind-set is one of the main secrets of my success. And I didn't get there easily. It almost seems as if my whole life has led to it. But now, every day, in every situation, I know I have the choice of perspective, and when I choose the side of hope and positivity, it feels good. I feel at home.

One afternoon, in 2018, some of the girls from work and I left the office and headed down to the ban.do parking lot, and right there next to my front-row parking spot was a mountain—a mountain!—of garbage. We all just stared at it, heads tilted, smirking at the fact that we were parking among this much trash. We were also aware of the irony that a company as bright and happy as ban.do would have two dumpsters filled with trash up to the ceiling. Our first instinct was to laugh, which in itself is a point of difference, because a group of pessimists would probably immediately feel anger and disgust. Not us. As the lead optimist,

I instantly felt compelled to dance in front of the trash and insisted Kelly film the whole thing so I could post all of this ridiculousness to Instagram. It's a little bit weird, I admit, that my first instinct while standing among overflowing dumpsters was to dance, but it speaks to where my mind goes when faced with something seemingly negative. I just thought the trash was funny, not depressing or gross. Once I posted it, the video gave people so much joy that it became the inaugural video of a regular feature of my Instagram Stories: Trashdance™.

Doing the running man in a basement parking lot with no regard for how crazy you look is silly and fun and incredibly freeing. My inclination to see the beauty even in the most garbage moments (literally) is a point of pride, I'll admit. Not because of my dance moves (spoiler alert: they're not that good) but because if I can see the upside (and the perfect dance backdrop) in a mountain of trash, then I can find the good in anything.

Acknowledgments

First and foremost, I want to send the biggest of thank-yous to you, the reader (or the bookstore-goer who just picked up this book and opened accidentally to this page—I hope you buy the book, read the book, and ultimately feel less alone by doing so). Thank you to all my friends for supporting me during this process, especially Busy, Kelly, and Ashley. You understood when I couldn't do much socializing for the better part of the year, you gave me advice when I needed it, and you celebrated with me when it was all done. Thank you to Lauren Spiegel for finding me so many years ago and then patiently waiting for me to be ready to write this book. And also for suggesting I go out to the desert to write when I was stuck—there

261

would be no Desert Jen without you. To Wylie O'Sullivan for getting me "unstuck" in the most gentle and loving way. For Monika Verma for being so patient and level-headed during all the sticking and unsticking. For Rachel Deitsche who came into my life and, more specifically, this book with what I am imagining is the largest well-functioning brain on the planet, then immediately dug in, making sense of it all (when a lot of it did not make sense) and ultimately shaping it into a great book. Jimmy, Jesse, Ashley (again), Jenn, Jordy, and Maddy for helping to create a book cover that feels like me, just with slightly shorter hair. Deb, you are my rock. Haha. I just always wanted to say that, but it's also true. You're a patient, organized angel from heaven, and I'm lucky to have you in my life. To my 7958 ban.do ride-or-dies—Kel, Ali, Natalie, Christina, and Tara, there would be no ban.do without you. You are more than friends, you are family, you live in my heart—and it's very cute in there. Todd and Kim Ferrier for buying ban.do but also for supporting me while I took a lot of time off work to go sit in the desert to write, although I mostly just cried and talked to inanimate objects. David Coffey, your friendship and partnership has meant the world to me, plus you're real and you're spectacular. To Jolie, you came into my life in the home stretch of this book and supported me in ways I didn't even know I needed—this is just the beginning. To Bettie for opening me up and healing what we found in there. Your guidance has value that transcends any number (even a gazillion). To Rich, you are a true gift. I'm sorry for breaking up with you when we were kids, but I'm glad you're back because I couldn't imagine life without you. To Andrew, although we aren't in each other's lives in the way we once were, I will always remain grateful for our love and our marriage. To Jason, who let the J out? Juh juh juh juhhhh! You escaped being in the book, except the tongue-in-your-mouth thing, sorry again for that, but you are a huge part of my life, one of my best friends, and I love you, well, like a brother, because you are my brother. And last but not least, Mom and Dad—Dr. Jamie and the Amazing Saerina. Thank you not only for being supportive and present parents for almost fifty years but also for honoring my desire to write this very personal book and for being so candid with me about your lives and your feelings and trusting me to share our experiences with lots and lots of strangers—I'm sure that was scary. I hope you know how brave you both are. I love you. Bye.

The Emotional Rating System

Throughout this book, I refer to my Emotional Rating System (ERS), a system I devised with my mom shortly after I got my depression diagnosis and moved to California. It was a good way for her to check in on my emotional state without requiring me to talk about my feelings, because when you're twenty-four, talking to your parents about your feelings can be incredibly annoying.

The ERS has helped me track and assess my moods, and it's an adaptable tool that provides an easy way to get in touch with how you're feeling at any given moment. I've adjusted it a bit over the years—when I got my proper bipolar diagnosis, it made sense to shift the ratings to identify both depression and hypomania—but it's a reliable system that enables anyone to gauge their emotional state, so I wanted to share.

The ERS is a simple scale of one to ten. Doctors often ask patients in the hospital to rate their pain on a scale of one to ten, and the ERS does the same, but instead of assigning a number to your pain, you're doing it for your mood.

On my scale, 1 is an extreme and dangerous low, and 10 reflects a hypomanic state. Anything 3 and below means I'm in a depressive episode, and even a 5 puts up a small red flag that I might be heading into a depression. Eight and above reflect an elevated mood, which feels very racy. And 7.8 is just right.

Here's what some of the most important points on the ERS look like for me—yes, I go down to the decimal. Moods are nuanced, and after you measure for a while you will actually be able to tell the difference between a 3.2 and a 3.6. (Keep in mind that everyone's scale is personal to them, so your 3.2, or 5, or 7.8 will look different—and feel different—than mine.)

1.9: I'm in the depths of depression. Not sad, just completely without emotion. Physically I can't move or talk. Not hungry. Not tired. It's like your soul went on vacation and you didn't get to go.

3.2: Still depressed, but usually from a situational catalyst. (The 1.9s tend to come out of nowhere.) I cry a lot. I'm agitated. I self-sooth with junk food, and I want to be alone!

5.0: It's not awful, it's just not right. It's like when you go to your favorite pizza place and the pizza isn't as good as you remember it, but you can't really say why. It's still pizza, so you're not mad or sad, just quietly yearning to feel satisfied.

7.8: The elusive 7.8! No depression, no mania. Food tastes good, but I can manage the emotional eating. I'm productive, happy, engaging, and alert. I'm funny, but not hysterical, and I look in the mirror and think, *Hey, you're okay!*

9.1: A 9.1 sounds fun (and it is), but it actually means I'm having a manic episode. The biggest signs are that I'm super talkative, love everyone, have a lot of energy, A LOT OF IDEAS, and I think I'm fucking incredible.

The ERS was incredibly helpful in getting to my accurate bipolar diagnosis, because after tracking my moods for several months, the numbers made it far easier for me, my psychiatrist, and my psychologist to draw conclusions.

Also, just like anything, the more you pay attention to it, the more you become aware of how you're feeling.

I know there are some great mood-tracking apps out there, but I like getting a piece of paper and writing 1 to 10 vertically, on the y axis, and then all the days of the month across the x axis. Put a dot where your mood is each day, and then connect them at the end. Mine looked far more like the Richter scale during an earthquake than a steady straight line (not that anyone's will be perfectly straight), and that's how we knew that there was a mood imbalance.

Tips for Using the ERS

As you're rating your emotions, think about the following three-step plan. It could help you glean valuable information as you track.

1. Acknowledge/identify/recognize
   - *What is happening in your life, your day, your mind?*
   - *How are you feeling about it?*

2. Process/evaluate
   - *Can you identify why this is happening?*
   - *What triggered you? (Did you introduce something new into your life? Did you get enough sleep?)*

3. Feel better (do something that makes you feel better and cope, or recognize situations you can avoid)
   - *Consider what your mind and body are really craving (exercise, sleep, quiet, fun). Accept your needs and cater to them without guilt.*

About the Author

Jen Gotch is genetically predisposed to optimism. A creative powerhouse and mental health advocate, she cofounded ban.do in 2008 and, with no prior business experience (and many people's help), transformed it from a small, vintage, one-of-a-kind hair accessories company into a multimillion-dollar brand. She hosted the Girlboss Radio autobiographical podcast *Jen Gotch is OK . . . Sometimes*, which focused on mental health, emotional intelligence, creative entrepreneurship, and the intersection of all three. Jen is passionate about sharing her experience in both business and life in a candid and lighthearted way in order to help others build their own self-awareness and emotional intelligence and most of all to help them feel less alone.